PENGUIN BOOK
In Search of Civiliz

Associate Professor John Armstrong is Philosopher in Residence at the Melbourne Business School and Senior Advisor to the Vice-Chancellor of Melbourne University. Born in Glasgow and educated at Oxford and London, he has lived in Australia since 2001. He is the author of several internationally acclaimed books on art, aesthetics and philosophy, including *The Secret Power of Beauty* and *Conditions of Love*.

JOHN ARMSTRONG
In Search of Civilization

Remaking a Tarnished Idea

PENGUIN BOOKS

PENGUIN BOOKS

Published by the Penguin Group
Penguin Books Ltd, 80 Strand, London WC2R ORL, England
Penguin Group (USA) Inc., 375 Hudson Street, New York, New York 10014, USA
Penguin Group (Canada), 90 Eglinton Avenue East, Suite 700, Toronto, Ontario, Canada M4P 2Y3
(a division of Pearson Penguin Canada Inc.)
Penguin Ireland, 25 St Stephen's Green, Dublin 2, Ireland
(a division of Penguin Books Ltd)
Penguin Group (Australia), 250 Camberwell Road, Camberwell, Victoria 3124, Australia
(a division of Pearson Australia Group Pty Ltd)
Penguin Books India Pvt Ltd, 11 Community Centre, Panchsheel Park, New Delhi – 110 017, India
Penguin Group (NZ), 67 Apollo Drive, Rosedale, North Shore 0632, New Zealand
(a division of Pearson New Zealand Ltd)
Penguin Books (South Africa) (Pty) Ltd, 24 Sturdee Avenue, Rosebank, Johannesburg 2196, South Africa

Penguin Books Ltd, Registered Offices: 80 Strand, London WC2R ORL, England

www.penguin.com

First published by Allen Lane 2009
Published in Penguin Books 2010
1

Copyright © John Armstrong, 2009
All rights reserved

Typeset by TexTech International
Printed in England by Clays Ltd, St Ives plc

ISBN: 978–0–141–03106–4

www.greenpenguin.co.uk

Penguin Books is committed to a sustainable future
for our business, our readers and our planet.
The book in your hands is made from paper
certified by the Forest Stewardship Council.

For William and Charlotte

Contents

PART THREE
Civilization as the Art of Living

PART FOUR
Civilization as Spiritual Prosperity

PART ONE
Civilization as Belonging

I

Bridget's Question

My desire to write about civilization took shape one evening while I was reading a bedtime story to my son. In Arthur Ransome's charming, low-key tale of childhood adventure *Secret Water* – part of the Swallows and Amazons series – the five Walker children leave their island camp on a sortie to the mainland. They are pretending to be savages. In the distance they see cottages and stubble fields, a line of telegraph poles; sunlight glints on a car windscreen: they are approaching an outpost of the civilized world.

'What is civilization?' asks Bridget, the youngest.

'Ices,' explains her brother Roger, 'and all that sort of thing.'

It is, perhaps, the briefest definition of the term in English.

If Roger's reply does not do justice to the idea of civilization, it serves at least to stimulate ambition. It is not just ice cream, so: What *is* civilization really?

The question expresses more than mild intrigue about the meaning of a word, such as one might feel about 'puce' or 'exiguous'. With the possible exception of God, civilization is the grandest, most ambitious idea that humanity has devised. If we could get to the heart of civilization and uncover its secret meaning, we would understand something deep and important about ourselves and the human condition and of urgent present relevance.

But the question 'What is civilization?' is bewildering. When we try to spell out the idea that the word points to we find ourselves at a loss. What are we to make of the fact that it is so hard to give a clear and potent answer? Does the difficulty we have defining civilization say something about the state of civilization?

Any great conceptual term, like 'justice', 'love' or 'civilization', collects a huge array of associations; they seem to mean too much. Civilization has *something* to do with cookery, insurance, technology, manners (as in 'civility'), geopolitics, art galleries, law, conversation, archaeology, personal hygiene, urban planning, ethics, science, shopping, religion, sex, poetry . . . Hence the anxiety when asked for a definition.

Our existing thoughts about terms like 'civilization' tend to be rather messy and muddled. And normally we don't worry about this. Philosophy invites us to be more demanding, more ambitious here; or, to put it negatively, to be less forgiving of our normal confusions.

What are the key ways 'civilization' is used? On some fantasy late-night discussion programme – today's approximation of a Socratic dialogue – four participants might each state a distinct line of thought connected with the word today.

The first panellist says that civilization names a collective scheme of values; a way of living: 'There are nine major civilizations in the world today. Islam, the West, China,

India and Russia are the largest; but there are plenty of smaller civilizations too: there is an Aboriginal civilization based in Outback Australia, with a very distinctive and ancient way of life. The civilization of Imperial Rome was the set of assumptions, patterns of behaviour and modes of thinking common to its citizens. A civilization is to do with what is shared and taken for granted by whole societies.' The speaker takes a sip of water and continues:

'A civilization structures the inner life of all those who belong to it. It shapes their sense of right and wrong, of what it is normal to eat, how to do business, what is noble or base, how to have a conversation or make a joke. To the insider these ways appear natural and obvious; to the outsider, baffling or intriguing. That's why there are such tensions between civilizations: the poetics of life are untranslatable.'

The second speaker disagrees. 'No,' they say: 'Civilization indicates a certain level of economic and political development. That's what we're getting at when we say things like civilization first developed along four river systems: the Nile, the Ganges, the Yellow River and in Mesopotamia, between the Tigris and the Euphrates. These were the first places where there was sufficient economic and political maturity to support towns and to undertake large-scale building projects. So civilization really refers to the technical capacities which a society has and the degree of social organization through which great collective effort is possible. Civilization is connected to the development and deployment of wealth and material power.

'This is how we generally speak. "We were driving in the hills, miles from civilization, when the gearbox gave way." That is, civilization is the sort of place you can find a garage. It's also what Gauguin must have had in mind when he said: "Civilization is poison" – he was taking a very negative view of modern urban life, business, technology and public administration. He was much happier away from it all and supposed everyone else would be too.'

There is a moment's pause; the third guest, who has been leaning back languidly, bends forward: 'Actually it's all to do with the sophisticated pursuit of pleasure. The cuisine and wines of Burgundy are among the triumphs of civilization. They offer rare delights to those who savour them. Civilization speaks with personal voice about the enjoyment, comfort and interest of life. It's much more to do with elegant bathrooms and well-stocked kitchens than museums. There's a minor character in *Anna Karenina* called Oblonsky – he's just ordered one of the best lunches in world literature – and he says: "the whole aim of civilization is to make everything a source of enjoyment". He's right. But I should perhaps use another example: the lunch is misleading because it's so expensive. A better example of what I mean by "civilization" would be a lovely little book by the French chef Edouard de Pomiane called *Cooking in Ten Minutes*. His recipes are extremely simple and cheap; what he's trying to do is teach people to enjoy a quick lunch; to have something nourishing and tasty, to order a little free time around cooking, eating, talking, listening to a piece of music. Money isn't the key factor here.'

Then the fourth person wades in. 'You're getting it all wrong. Surely, civilization requires a high level of intellectual and artistic excellence: the Louvre, for instance, is a temple to civilization because you can see so many of the most esteemed works of art. Civilization doesn't indicate what is normal in a society; it picks out the grandest, most noble achievements. These are always atypical. Do you remember Kenneth Clark's series from the late 1960s? He kept talking about civilization as the history of "life-giving ideas" – well he certainly didn't mean the most popular ideas; he thought the most civilized place ever was the Renaissance court of Urbino – where a few dozen people developed an amazingly elegant mode of existence.

'I'm one of those people who always tends to see civilization as being in decline: "It's closing time in the gardens of the West"; "The lamps are going out." That's not the worry that people aren't going to have dishwashers or hospital beds; it's the worry that the finest flowers of culture are too delicate and too refined to survive.'

These could be seen as four independent, equally valid, opinions about civilization. Inspired by Socrates, there is a tradition of thought that seeks to unravel the varied meanings that have become entangled around a word. This tradition laments the occasions when a single term, such as 'civilization', is used indiscriminately to signal quite different concerns. Four meanings, one word: confusion is certain to follow. Thinking is an art of separation: you isolate and inspect the different strands. Perhaps there is no central meaning of civilization, no essence, just a sequence of different definitions. (On this view, Bridget will have to be patient and listen to four answers to her question.)

Last summer, I was having a weekend lunch with a friend; we were chatting about this book. 'Are you going to tell the history of lots of different civilizations' – she brushed away a fly; we were eating in her garden – 'or are you going to concentrate on a particular period?' I was not planning to do either. A very understandable tendency of thought was revealed by this friend's question. Her idea of getting to know an idea is to pile up more and more historical and sociological information. Probably she was half recalling some of the leading books about the topic.

For instance, in 1860 Jacob Burckhardt – one of the founding fathers of modern art history – published a book called *The Civilization of the Renaissance in Italy*. In it he tries to identify the underlying aspirations of those times: a growing concern with individuality, a tendency to see the state as a work of art: internally unified and self-aware. He investigates what was going on in a particular region at a particular time and does not in fact have much to say about the idea of civilization itself (or – to be strictly accurate – about the German term 'Kultur', which appears in the original title and is only approximately translated as 'civilization'). Instead he works with the reasonable assumption that Renaissance Italy is an interesting example of civilization and then tells us about it.

A similar approach is evident in many tomes brought out in a grand series by the art publishers Thames & Hudson, with titles like *Maya Civilization*, *American Civilization*, *Angkor and the Khmer Civilization*, all of which tell us a great deal about these different societies and their cultural achievements; but they do not discuss the idea of civilization itself.

I could not at that moment, while coping with an oyster, pull together much of an explanation of what I was going to do, or why. What I want to do is understand the core idea of civilization. So the examples I employ are not intended to tell the story of any particular society, or characterize its culture at any particular time. Rather, they are intended to illustrate distinctions or convey concepts. I have been looking for representative occasions when a particular theme or issue comes to the fore.

My friend at lunch was trying to saddle me with the task of discovering what other people have thought about civilization. Whereas what motivates me is something more personal: What do I think? To put it another way, I want to move from asking the historical question about how people happen to have defined civilization to the philosophical question about how we ought to define it.

The historical question is quite difficult: you have to search about in all sorts of books to find out how people have used this particular word and try to reconstruct the context in which it acquired meaning. But the philosophical project faces difficulties of a different kind. It is harder to work out what you think, and why, than to investigate what another person has thought. It is harder to judge which meaning is most important than to record variations in use. But the harder task is also very much more important. After all, what is the point of finding out about what other people think? It is a prelude to discovering your own ideas.

2

'Wider Still and Wider'

The discussion described on the imagined chat show is not very likely to occur. Not because the speakers do not interrupt one another but because civilization is not at present a fashionable topic of intellectual discussion. A few years ago I attended a conference in London organized by the Getty Institute, the exceptionally wealthy cultural foundation that supports the study of art and art history. There was a session devoted to the topic of civilization. The conference was held in Somerset House, one of the finest neoclassical buildings in the world. (It has wonderful staircases.)

That morning, three eminent academic figures presented papers. The main theme was that civilization could no longer be regarded as a particularly important idea. They were perfectly aware of the common uses of the term. But none of these – in the eyes of the speakers – held much intellectual promise. They were not making a radical or novel claim; they were restating a long-standing orthodoxy. From my ten years of intellectual apprenticeship in philosophy and the history of art, from 1986 to 1996, I could not recall any occasion on which the word 'civilization' had been mentioned. In 2001 the events of 11 September had – it is true – given a new life to the word through the idea of a clash of civilizations. But this was seen as a debate within international politics, of no real relevance to the study of art or philosophy or to the conduct of everyday life.

The root of the problem appeared to be that the idea of civilization had kept bad company. It had been eagerly invoked to justify colonial expansion. A dramatic instance of this attitude can be found in the words of 'Land of Hope and Glory', powerfully set to the music of the best known of Elgar's *Pomp and Circumstance Marches* and first performed in 1902 as part of the celebrations for the Coronation of Edward VII:

> Wider still and wider shall thy bounds be set,
> God, who made thee mighty [orchestra swells here], make thee mightier yet.

Taking the words and music together, it is an ensemble saturated with glorification of empire and dominion, but experienced entirely from the point of view of the overlords.

The view that industrially developed countries had a mission to rule less-developed societies – and not merely an opportunity for increased wealth and power based on physical might – was facilitated by deployment of the term 'civilization'. Civilization carries a moral implication: a civilized society is better than an uncivilized one; civilized life is fully human: noble and wise. But it also carries a suggestion of superior material development: more factories, more guns. Whole nations could convince themselves that they had a moral right to lordship over other lands, mistaking material superiority for moral legitimacy.

The 'make thee mightier yet' portrait presents civilization as an historical and psychological problem: an attitude of arrogance and self-congratulation. The conclusion seemed plain. The idea of civilization should be dropped. The conference was a kind of funeral service for an idea that had had its – not very admirable – day.

After the session I went for a walk along the nearby Thames Embankment. I was rather depressed. I could not disagree with the analysis of the unfortunate uses to which the idea of civilization had been put. But I felt there was some finer and still relevant significance locked up in the word. Any term, however well intentioned in its origins, can be diverted to malign purposes. But that only makes more urgent the task of separating what is valuable and important in the idea of civilization from the false and misleading uses to which the word has been put.

As I wandered about, I thought of a story told by the Roman poet Ovid in the *Metamorphoses* – the book of changes, as we might call it – which I felt provided an analogy for my worry. A young couple, recently married, are much in love. As the husband says: 'We were equally in love, cared equally for one another.' The lovely wife gives her husband a present: a new javelin. At dawn, 'when the first rays struck the hilltops', the husband set off hunting. His wife follows and lies down among the bushes. By chance the husband is near and, hearing a leaf fall, he imagines a wild beast is close by. He hurls his new javelin and – of course – it strikes his wife. And so, by mistaking her, he causes her death.

It is a complex, strange story in the full telling. But the thing that stayed in my mind was simple. It was the image of someone inadvertently damaging the very thing they love because they fail to recognize it. In the magnificent lecture room, I had witnessed the hurling of javelins. But what had been hit? My fear was that, thinking that the idea of civilization was a threat, the speakers had launched their darts. But my suspicion was that something precious was hidden in the bushes; that seen, more clearly, the idea of civilization might turn out to be something we need and love.

The conference revealed something that is of central importance. Some of the people one might naturally have looked to as keepers of the flame of civilization – as people especially well placed to foster civilization – had neglected this task. They had taught themselves to be wary and negative. Although civilization is a social and political concept, its native centre is to be found in the arts and humanities. These are – I believe – the deepest foundations of civilization, although what gets built on those foundations reaches out in every possible direction. What I was witnessing at the conference was not just another mildly diverting academic discussion. It was a glimpse into the state of the foundations of civilization; and the sight was extremely worrying.

In order to unlock the potential of civilization – to recognize it for what it is – we need to embark upon a philosophical discussion. The problem is not that we lack information or facts about our own or previous societies. It is not that we do not know enough about those past and present societies that are called civilizations. The key discussion has to start in another place: it should be around what we mean by civilization – what our idea of civilization is. More ambitiously, it should focus on the question: What *should* our idea of civilization be? We are not merely passive receptors of existing strategies of thinking. Philosophy is the project of discovering and creating the ideas we need.

For me, philosophy is an intimate project. I want to

understand freedom *when* I feel limited and oppressed. I want to make sense of the value of art *when* others praise something I loath, or *when* I love a work but find it hard to say why. And that, in turn, makes me curious about the nature of love and loathing.

Bridget's simple query, 'What is civilization?', struck me powerfully because it connected up to deep-set memories, fears and hopes. 'Civilization' has always been – for me – the name of something longed for: the place of refuge and happiness. It has never been connected, in my experience, to oppression or boredom – as I imagine it might have been in the lives of the speakers at the conference. No one has ever bothered me or troubled me in the name of civilization.

Perhaps we are inescapably marked – when it comes to ideas – by early life, when experience is particularly raw and ideas fresh. My deepest fear is of loutish bullying and, close second, of appealing for help and being told the problem lies in me. Uncritical emphasis upon ideas like difference and equality is terrifying. 'The shopping-centre car park isn't ugly – just different, so stop howling.' 'You aren't any better than this mocking vulgarian – so get off your high horse.' I want to bite off my hand in impotent rage.

The word 'civilization' carries an aura of grace, dignity, good order, security: qualities that I longed for, but which were not conspicuous or strong in the world in which I grew up. And it is this longing that explains (I now think) my distress at the conference. As if I were being told – in the politest and most erudite way – that what I love is not important.

3

The Clash of Civilizations

I want to look in more detail at the four sketches of civilization gleaned from the imagined chat show. Picking up on the first of these: 'civilization' is often used in connection with a political thesis. The epic phrase 'the clash of civilizations' has influenced the way major international conflicts of our times are imagined.

There is a grand narrative that goes like this: During the period of the Cold War the geopolitical map was divided ideologically into the Free World and the Communist Bloc. Most countries had to stand in one line or the other making, at times, strange companions. Afghanistan was aligned with the Free World, not because of any deep affinity, but because it was engaged in fighting Soviet forces.

With the end of the Cold War, in the final years of the 1980s, this way of seeing the world became obsolete; a crisis of identity ensued. Instead of Capitalism versus Communism, the world divided up according to a very different sort of loyalty: a loyalty premised on civilizations.

In the book that made the running on this issue, *The Clash of Civilizations*, Samuel P. Huntington put it like this: 'In coping with an identity crisis, what counts for people are blood and belief, faith and family.'

Civilization comes in here because it provides the largest

shell of identification. It yields the biggest answer to the basic questions: Who are you? Where do you belong? Who is your friend and who your enemy? Much of the time, our concerns about who we are have a local flavour: they are to do with positioning ourselves among the people we encounter day by day. But in a time of globalization, very large-scale answers to the root questions of identity and belonging become more significant.

At the global level you will see yourself and be seen as belonging to a particular civilization. Civilizations in this sense are long-standing, widespread visions of life: ways of shaping, explaining and ordering experience. A civilization usually develops around a linguistic, religious and regional core. It is drawn together by collective memory of shared exposure to the large rhythms of history.

In the language of rapid approximation, the West has in common something like this: the countries that constitute the West evolved out of the Roman Empire and share a cultural tradition of classicism. The Senate Square in Helsinki employs a similar visual vocabulary to the public buildings in Washington and Melbourne. (The construction of St Petersburg along neoclassical lines was a gesture of westernization.)

The religious roots of the West are Judaeo-Christian, with many bloody tensions around the interpretation of that heritage. The West, as a whole, encountered industrialization and its problems earlier than any other part of the world. These states were, in general, colonizers rather than the colonized from the sixteenth to the twentieth century. Somewhere in the mix is a moderately robust attachment to individual freedom and rational, sceptical inquiry. For the last five hundred years the West has driven technological, scientific and commercial innovation.

These are 'commonalities' of the West: the loose set of assumptions and associations that are recognizable in places otherwise as different as Portugal and Denmark, Dorset and California. The communalities of a civilization create a shared identity. Of course, the kinds of answers given in the civilizations of India or China or Islam are very different. But however the answers differ, they play the same role: they help explain who you are.

So an individual belongs to a civilization not just by being at some particular spot on the surface of the planet, but in an intimate way that is often unconscious unless an external force provokes recognition.

Through the main body of his work Huntington argues that understanding certain major geopolitical tensions requires reference to civilizations. His central examples of such tensions are drawn from the Balkans and the Middle East. A crucial component of these conflicts is loyalty focused on the civilizational themes of religion and race, often seeking to restructure nations in line with these loyalties. Such loyalty adds intensity to any conflict and is an obstacle to pragmatic compromise. Across the boundaries of civilization, trust diminishes, communication becomes difficult; misunderstandings arise and perspectives diverge.

This is an organic conception of civilization. It suggests that everything that makes up a civilization is tightly interwoven. You are born into a way of life – the structures of meaning you come to see as natural and normal are, themselves, the root and expression of a set of values and traditions of behaviour. What you eat, how you prepare it, what it is to be a friend, what the duties of parents are, how you tell a story, how you dress, what the distinctions between adults and children are, what is considered honourable or shameful – all of these deep features of existence are woven into a civilization, and to belong to a civilization is to participate naturally in them. But, of course, the very things that bind an individual to a civilization also form a horizon of understanding. If you have to be brought up in a civilization and have to experience it from the inside in order to belong to it, then the basis on which you can understand another civilization is quite limited. That is why the boundaries between civilizations are those across which it is difficult for trust and sympathy to jump.

Thus, if we want to grasp why the conflicts between Israel and Palestine or Russia and America are so complex and long-standing, we have to take into account the factor of civilization. The deepest assumptions about how one should live, about what an acceptable form of government might be, or what makes a life worth living are divergent. At worst the other civilization looks pointless. As if one simply cannot make sense of what the other actually wants, or why it might seem so hard for them to compromise or to be reasonable – by one's own standard of rationality.

Having elaborated all this, Huntington ends up suggesting that 'the real clash' is actually between civilization and barbarism. 'The world's great civilizations with their rich accomplishments in religion, art, literature, philosophy, science, technology, morality and compassion' are natural collaborators, not natural enemies. Understood this way, the world's civilizations will 'hang together or hang separately': they will flourish in harmony or die.

There seems to be a paradox here. On the one hand, we have the distinctive 'commonalities' of each civilization; divergence of these commonalities generates conflict, distrust, and makes communication difficult. On the other hand, the 'rich accomplishments' of different civilizations are proposed as natural collaborators. The puzzle is that the commonalities look very like the rich accomplishments. So the same traditions of experience and value play contradictory roles: now pushing civilizations apart, now drawing them together.

Mahatma Gandhi once made a comment that helps dissolve this apparent paradox. Asked what he thought of Western civilization he said, 'It would be a very good thing.' At first sight this is absurd. Obviously the West has its commonalities. And it is not as if the West is lacking in rich accomplishments. But Gandhi was not suggesting that Plato, Jesus, Galileo, Mozart, Thomas Jefferson, Goethe and Einstein were frauds and fools. The point was, surely, that their achievements and best spirit had not penetrated and guided the thought and behaviour of anything like enough people.

In other words, you might well see yourself as belonging to a civilization, but that does not on its own make you civilized.

The first sketch of civilization as a set of shared beliefs brings two issues into focus. One is a matter of quantity. Civilization depends upon widespread, shared conceptions of life. The full concept of civilization needs to retain this sense of common life and the powerful experience of belonging to a society. The second issue concerns quality. Civilization does not merely endorse whatever happens to be the accepted currency of assumption; it aims at the best version – the version that is most intelligent – of a particular tradition of experience. Civilization depends upon how *good* the widespread conception of life is; or, to put it another way, how *widespread* the good conception is.

There is often a painful split: it seems as though loyalty becomes common and widespread only when it betrays the rich accomplishments to which it pays lip service, while the real nature of these accomplishments is appreciated by a relatively small number of people.

The attempt to draw these two concerns together – and to make what is best also what is shared, to align quantity and quality – is a key element in the civilizing process. This is the process whereby a civilization in the less ambitious sense of the term becomes civilized according to a more ambitious meaning.

As we become more civilized as individuals – as we appreciate the worth of ideas, as we become more subtle and refined, as we distinguish more carefully between degrees of importance – we leave behind the official loyalties of our society, which function in a more coarse and unambitious way. Ideally, we gain – through this development – membership of a more elusive but still real community: the community of civilized people.

4

Quality of Relationships

The distinction between qualities of attachment is of great importance; but it is also rather delicate. To get a closer sense of what is at stake, consider a specific and comparatively minor instance of the clash of religious loyalties that plagued the West. For a long time, the population of Scotland was divided along sectarian lines. There was something very interesting, as well as unpleasant, about this split. It offers a microcosm in which we can examine loyalty and draw conclusions that are significant for the much larger topic of the clash of civilizations – and ultimately will reveal something important about the idea of civilization itself.

Taken seriously, the Catholic and Protestant versions of Christianity are profound, if imperfect, achievements. In their way each is wise and sensitive. Protestantism at its best is grounded in an intense awareness of the drama of the individual conscience and takes a cautious approach to symbols. Catholicism at its best is grounded in an appreciation of the grandeur and depth of symbols and takes a cautious approach to the individual intellect as a guide to life.

Even a sectarian bigot, on either side, is in some sense loyal to and proud of their religion. The object of their loyalty is, if properly understood and appreciated, a set of noble and serious concerns – whether factually correct or not. But in the lives and minds of many people religion is not properly understood or appreciated. The real point of believing has been lost. This is brought out by posing the questions: 'Why are you loyal to this religion? What is it you actually believe?' To which one would get – at worst – answers like: 'I was born to the faith'; 'I hate the Pope'; 'Protestants are scum.' But these cannot possibly be reasons to believe such detailed and defining doctrines as the forgiveness of sin by the grace of God, or that the Eucharist is a memorial service, not an evocation of the real presence of Christ. Someone can feel intensely loyal, no matter how big the gap between their conception of their religion and its defining doctrines.

Such a person takes hold of a rich accomplishment but in a way that has no grip on the real merit of the ideas and practices at stake. Loyalty – as with liking and admiration – has an 'intentional' object. That is, you are loyal not so much to a person or an institution or an idea as they really are but to the way you imagine and think about that person, institution or idea.

Someone loyal to what is good in Protestantism, who has absorbed its emphasis upon individual conscience and adhered to its roots in charity and meekness, could not easily become a crude and cruel bigot. Just as someone who has adhered to what is good in Catholicism and has absorbed its devotion to love and forgiveness would be armed against vicious prejudice. This hopeful scenario has in fact been borne out in a remarkably clear way. In Scotland, during the past thirty years, there has been a very widespread reduction in religious observance. Those who continue to identify strongly with a particular Christian denomination do so, almost always, on serious and intimate spiritual grounds. They seek as best they can wisdom, love, forgiveness and transcendent meaning. They are not just acting out accidental allegiances: the consequence of having been bred in one faction or another. The consequence has been a powerful and stable rapprochement between denominations.

The same point can be made of loyalty to civilizations. The rich accomplishments of China, Islam or the West are not really in desperate conflict. And the more someone is loyal to what is genuinely fine about any one of these achievements the more respect they would have for what is finest in the others. For example, in a delightful book written in the 1940s entitled *The Silent Traveller in Edinburgh* (part of an extensive series of travel essays), Chiang Yee, a senior administrator in China in the 1930s, is able to discover an extraordinary community of interest between the culture he has deeply absorbed in his Mandarin education and the culture he discovers in the finest cities of the West. Or consider *The Book of Tea* by Kakuzo Okakura, first published in 1906, which is profoundly suggestive for the understanding of how an activity becomes an art and, hence, of the civilizing process.

Such points and examples support Huntington's final claim. What is best in each civilization has much in common; more in common, in fact, than with degraded versions of itself. The rich achievements of any civilization are not in violent conflict, and in fact are on the same side in a clash between cultivated intelligence and barbarism. The irony is that such barbarism too often goes under the name of loyalty to a civilization.

*

True civilization is constituted by high-quality relationships to ideas, objects and people. The quality of a relationship depends upon the contribution of both parties. What does the other person, idea or object really offer me? And how do I engage with what is offered: what do I bring to the relationship?

A good relationship with a person cannot be formed if the other party has nothing of true worth to offer. If the other person is sour, cynical, dogmatic and inattentive you cannot form a high-quality relationship to them – the good things you might bring have nowhere to go in that person. You can pour out all you have to offer and it will come to nothing. This is particularly sad and dangerous when the other person possesses the superficial marks of worth: they appear sexy or knowing, they have money, glamour or high status. In that case we are pulled in by the surface appeal; but no good relationship can be formed because, beneath the surface, there is nothing for our love to engage with.

Something very similar can be seen in our relationships with objects and ideas. Think of the phrase: 'You can see the world in a grain of sand.' That is true only if you imaginatively project the richness of the world into the unpromising object. It is not really there to be seen. The grain contributes almost nothing: you have to do all the work. It is a metaphor for a very one-sided and unreal relationship.

Across the road from the café where I often go in the afternoons there is a large hospital building from the 1970s. Of course I'm glad that big hospitals exist, but the building is one that repels visual attention. I can understand it as an historical and economic phenomenon: the bland international modernist style in which it is built happened to be the cheapest mode of construction available. It occupies a whole city block: grim and domineering. It has nothing to say to any desire for grace or dignity.

Or consider ideas: one can develop an obsession with certain propositions. 'Beauty is a myth constructed to sell cosmetics'; 'America is evil'; 'I will be happy if I buy a new car'; 'Everything unnatural is bad'; 'We must innovate or die.' I do not even want to mention the truly appalling ideas – about race and sexuality – that have, at times, captured widespread loyalty.

Such ideas may grip the imagination of an individual. But one cannot form a high-quality relationship to them. Tenderness, intelligence, curiosity and imagination have nowhere to go. You have to leave those qualities behind in order to maintain the obsession.

These are cases in which a high quality of relationship cannot occur because the person or thing we are attempting to relate to does not bring enough into the relationship.

Equally, a high quality of relationship does not emerge simply because I am in the presence of a wonderful person, a deep and important idea or a noble and fine object. I may not be able to attend to, learn from or appreciate what the other person has to offer. Their merits, however real, are lost on me. I may experience the delicacy of another person's behaviour as posing; I may hear insight as pretension; I may consider tenderness to be sentimentality. The problem lies with me. As the merits of the other person enter my consciousness they are cut down and humiliated, stripped of their true character and made to fit the limited template of my mind. This is the secret of prejudice: it is not discrimination but an inability to recognize the merits of another person.

There is a comment by the nineteenth-century art critic and social reformer John Ruskin that speaks to this point. He says: A book does me no good if I cannot read it; nor if I can read it but not understand it, nor if I can understand it but not assimilate it to my life. He is thinking of the case in which I lack the capacity to recognize and use the merits of an idea. Even the grandest thoughts can become trivial for us if we have trivial minds. The idea that 'beauty lies in the eye of the beholder' can be infinitely deep and serious – because it hints at the importance of receptivity. But it can be taken in a trivial and damaging way: beauty is just a name for whatever someone happens to like. The potential of the thought is lost. A scientific notion like relativity, which says nothing at all about the human condition, can be used as if it were a theory not of the structure of the universe but an ethical principle: 'Because relativity is true, there is no such thing as moral truth.'

I may be pacing the courts and galleries of the Louvre, surrounded by many of the finest creative achievements of humanity, but receive from them only low-grade surprise and confirmation of my existing assumptions: the *Mona Lisa* is smaller than one would have thought; almost all old paintings were painted for rich people, therefore they are essentially snobbish objects. The larger potential of the object finds no recognition, no home, in me.

Civilization is the life-support system for high-quality relationships to people, ideas and objects: it feeds and sustains love ('love' is the one-word version of the phrase 'high quality of relationship'). In genuine love we do not only have an appetite for and devotion to something or someone, but we also perceive what is good and loveable and recognize our own need to meet and engage with that.

The life-support system for love has two aspects. First, civilization seeks to find and protect the good things with which – potentially – we can form high-quality relationships. And, second, civilization fosters and protects the qualities in us that allow us to love such things for the right reasons. The qualities that inspire love are: goodness, beauty and truth. And when we love these qualities we come to possess the corresponding capacities of wisdom, kindness and taste.

Because quality of relationship is a matter of degree, even degraded, low-quality relationships have some weak kinship with what they ought to be. They are impoverished, limited versions of finer connections. Greed is the beginner's version of appreciation – where taking in a great deal of something is imagined to be the way of getting what you need. Vulgarity – getting excited by money and a famous name – is a beginner's guide to love; it is the search for a meaningful point of contact, only it is unable to imagine what intimate and real engagement is like. Somewhere within many silly or dangerous ideas, there is a significant truth lurking in a coarse, exaggerated and alienated guise.

Love is the antidote to fashion and gossip; for love spurns rapid change; it repudiates the language (and the inner attitude that fuels the words) of what is 'hot' or what is 'in'. Love spurns trivia – or, better, longs for what is real and substantial.

5

The Paradox of Freedom

In cultivating high-quality relationships, we become better versions of ourselves. Such relationships bring out, and feed, one's best self.

This phrase, the 'best self', comes from a series of lectures delivered in 1867 by the poet and critic Matthew Arnold during his tenure as Professor of Poetry at Oxford. The position was an honorary one and Arnold earned his living as an inspector of schools. The lectures were later published under the title *Culture and Anarchy*. The date is significant. In 1867 the Second Reform Bill was passed in Britain, widely extending the franchise. Until then, voting rights had been restricted to men who owned property of substantial value. Now a much larger portion of the adult male population had a say in the political life of Britain. (Although some men and almost all women had to wait until 1928.)

Arnold was by no means opposed to this reform. But he was troubled by it. The cause of his anxiety is given in his most famous poem, 'Dover Beach' – one of the finest pieces of English writing. It ends with the words:

> . . . the world, which seems
> To lie before us like a land of dreams,

So various, so beautiful, so new,
Hath really neither joy, nor love, nor light,
Nor certitude, nor peace, nor help for pain;
And we are here as on a darkling plain
Swept with confused alarms of struggle and flight,
Where ignorant armies clash by night.

Arnold thought that ignorant armies had always been clashing by night; but the extension of voting rights was liable to increase the confusion. This was a period when the popular press was coming into powerful existence; it was an age too of great public rallies with fiery speeches; there was a multiplication of religious sects, each claiming that its path was the only true one. That is why even in small country towns in Britain and Australia there are sometimes six or seven different large church buildings – each representing a different denomination – all dating from the second half of the nineteenth century.

These, in Arnold's view, were forces of anarchy: the ignorant armies clashing in the dark. It was not that he thought there should not be newspapers or religion (although he was personally sceptical) or political movements or widespread democracy. Nor did he think that the previous state of society was admirable: he was a social reformer. He was worried that the developments taking place in the name of reform and progress were not actually beneficial, at least not in the form they were taking. Each faction, newspaper, sect or interest group sought to win adherents and to demonize its enemies. Each tended to stick to its own limited and particular view of life and of the problems of the world.

This is essentially the problem of liberty: freedom to 'do as one likes' so long as there is no infringement of the rights of others. The achievement of political liberty and the legal framework that supports it is clearly very impressive. But Arnold saw the triumph of liberty as posing – in ever more stark terms – questions that the doctrine of liberty could not itself answer. Liberty says it is up to you to work out your own destiny, to decide what to believe and why, to create and follow your own vision of life. And that only restates, and does not solve, the question of what a good life consists in. The success of liberalism makes more acute the question of value and purpose that it now places in the hands of individuals.

Arnold is our contemporary in his thinking. The problems that so concerned him: how to educate freedom, how to give people the strength to use freedom well, are issues that have become more acute since he delivered his lectures. Arnold is so important to the discussion of civilization because he is analysing and responding to some major obstacles to flourishing that were coming into view during his life and which have only grown in significance since.

This is the crisis of freedom and power: the freedom of the individual and the rapidly developing technical and commercial environment in which that freedom is exercised. These problems came together in Arnold's England because it saw simultaneously the Industrial Revolution and the opening up of democracy. The crisis comes about because democracy and technology are so valuable to us: they vastly extend the possibilities of human flourishing. Yet at the same time they can be obstacles to flourishing. Each has tended to endorse the ordinary self, so that freedom becomes merely the right to 'do as one likes'.

Arnold saw each factional group as expressing the 'ordinary self' of its adherents. They address the prejudices and obsessions of their audience, confirming and entrenching limitations and deficiencies; in fact, the purpose of such groups is to tell people that what they happen to think already – what they happen to find appealing – is what is truly important in life.

Civilization aims to make us wise, kind and tasteful. It seeks to provide us with a human community, an intellectual arena and a physical environment in which wisdom, kindness and taste are at home.

Civilization has to be pursued in the world as we have it. Three particular features of modernity may be seen – in a pessimistic light – as making civilization either impossible or no longer desirable. We have liberal economic markets. If you can pay, you can have what you want so long as you do not break the law. Whether your choices are good or bad is for you to decide, and you can pursue them until you run out of credit. Therefore the market says: I do not care about quality of choice or whether people consume wisely. I care about whether or not they can pay for whatever it is they happen to want.

We have cultural democracy. Who is to say what sort of art or books or architecture I should like? Everyone's preference is on an equal footing. Some people like Beethoven, some Britney, others both. In the past, elites could trumpet their preferences as superior; they were the only ones in a position to do any trumpeting. Today there is little cultural authority – there is little deference.

We have freedom of opinion. I am entitled to think whatever I happen to think – irrespective of logic, evidence and self-examination – so long as it doesn't directly and obviously harm other people. No one has any right to tell me what to think. Such freedom is rooted in the profound point that the truths we discover for ourselves are more valuable than those we merely accept on external authority. One is expected to have strong opinions on the widest range of baffling technical matters and impacted problems: the state of the planet; how to bring peace and justice to the Middle East; how the economy can be put to rights; the relationship between science and religious faith. The quality of information on which we base our opinions may be low and the quantity slight. But we are perfectly entitled to our own views.

These conditions are associated with a pessimistic view of civilization today. Triumphant vulgarity rules the world (it is said) because the democratic numbers and the market forces always win. Once you have markets, cultural democracy and freedom of opinion, questions about merit and meaning will always be settled by majorities and money. But majorities and money have no real authority on questions of value.

But these conditions cannot be essentially hostile to civilization. They are all manifestations of freedom. They act out the principle that evaluations lie in the hands of individuals and should not be forced, because – when forced – they are no longer authentic, and it is essential to evaluation that it should be authentic. You cannot be forced to love or admire or believe. The qualities of relationship that I have been pointing to – wisdom, kindness and taste – all grow with freedom.

Freedom is not in opposition to civilization, rather, freedom is the most demanding arena in which civilization is played out; the greater the freedom we have, the greater our need for civilization. The greater the potential – in liberty, wealth and technology – the greater the organizing force needs to be to lead that potential to fruition.

The optimistic analysis goes like this: freedom and markets do not entail anarchy. They reflect the condition of most people: the majority of 'ordinary selves' – to draw again on Matthew Arnold's vocabulary. The work of civilization is to speak to the ordinary self of its longing to become the best version of itself. What is finest in the history of a civilization is not arbitrary. Its worth is intimate and permanent: it offers something wonderful to most people – if only what is wonderful and good in it could be made more apparent, if only the need for it could be more easily recognized. The civilizing mission is to make what is genuinely good more readily available and to awaken an appetite for it.

For most of the twentieth century, the discussion and pursuit of love – for ideas and objects – appeared neither cool nor clever; this was for quite serious reasons. Love cannot appear knowing and detached; it cannot disown tenderness and sorrow; it is vulnerable and individual; hence it is at odds with superficial social allure. Also, love – however much fed by insight and understanding – is not finally an intellectual relationship.

The project for civilization today can be formulated like this: it is the encouragement, support and protection of high-quality relationships to ideas, objects and other people undertaken in the arena of freedom. Telling people what to do, making rules and regulations are only strategies for addressing fairly gross needs (which of course are of great importance). You cannot tell someone what to love. And yet, many people know how great, and how real, help can be.

6

The Best Self

The aim of *Culture and Anarchy* was to provide a solution to this state of affairs. The current value of Arnold's work lies in the fact that the world today exhibits extreme versions of the problems with which he was concerned. His suggestion is this: we need to 'get to know, on the matters that most concern us, the best that has been thought and said in the world; and through this knowledge, turn a stream of fresh and free thought upon our stock notions and habits, which we now follow staunchly but mechanically, vainly imagining that there is a virtue in following them staunchly which makes up for the mischief of following them mechanically.'

The antidote to factionalism is the free play of thought: wondering whether one might be mistaken, considering whether a favoured personal position is merely a prejudice, or whether it is really wise. It is not so much that Arnold wants to impose his own set of opinions; he is arguing for mental space, for hesitance and reflection. And he wants to feed into this mental space 'the best that has been thought and said in the world' – for stimulation, guidance and comparison, and not as a source of new dogmas.

In embryo, the 'best self' is the appetite for self-improvement along these lines: a willingness to consider, reflect and wonder; and, in its full sense, the result of giving this a central and continuing place in existence. He gave this ideal the name of Hellenism, in part because he was inspired by the character of the Greek philosophers – particularly Socrates. He admired the way Socrates sat about in the market place or down by the harbour questioning, arguing and patiently exploring ideas. Socrates represents the spirit of self-examination and free inquiry: How do you know? Are you sure? What are the alternatives? This approach was what was lacking in the hectoring certainties Arnold thought of as characteristic of his own times.

Such a questioning spirit, however, is only one aspect of Hellenism. There is a positive aspect that is just as important. 'To get rid of one's ignorance, to see things as they are, and by seeing them as they are to see them in their beauty, is the simple and attractive ideal which Hellenism holds out before human nature; and from the simplicity and charm of this ideal, Hellenism, and human life in the hands of Hellenism, is invested with a kind of aerial ease, clearness and radiancy; they are full of what we call sweetness and light.' This is Arnold's picture of the best self – of how we could and should be.

At the time, Arnold's critics tended to see him as impractical; and they were right, as he acknowledged. But the ease with which the charge was made led Arnold to think of it as unimportant. Practicality, he thought, could largely take care of itself; the energy to get things done, to make money, to be in charge of things, to impose one's will on others was not exactly in short supply. So there was little need to say that, of course, the ideal of Hellenism needs to be supplemented with attention to practical matters; it is rather that the widespread human tendency to be occupied with practical matters needs to be supplemented by this ideal.

Arnold intimates the limitation of practicality with a code word: 'machinery'. A machine allows you to work faster, to make more of something, to operate on a larger scale. But these matters do not touch upon the fundamental questions: Why is this product good? Are we doing the right thing? Is it wise to move in this direction? In Arnold's sense, mobile phones are 'machinery': they allow us to communicate more often, to take more photographs, to locate restaurants; but these resources do not automatically help us reach the 'ends' they ideally serve: good conversation, deep relationships, convivial evenings, the appreciation of beauty. But it is normal to be deeply impressed by technical capacity and to leave the 'ends' – the really important bits – to look after themselves. A more acute analysis would run in the opposite direction: we should concentrate on 'ends' (beauty, good conversation, deep relationships) and the 'means' will not be lacking.

It was the cultivation of the spirit of Hellenism – and hence of the best self – that, Arnold thought, was absolutely necessary to counteract preoccupation with machinery and the clamorous fragmentation that came with democracy, interest-group politics, opinionated newspapers, sects and subcultures. The idea was not that the cultivation of Hellenism would do away with human disagreement, but rather that it would change the character of that disagreement. It does this by transforming the character of attachment to ideas: making it at once more flexible and more intelligent. More intelligent because grounded in awareness of 'the best that has been thought and said', and more flexible because the topics on which dissention arises are, almost always, matters of speculation rather than matters of fact. And the more one sees speculation for what it is, the more one's adherence becomes fluid.

Arnold's passion was for 'diffusing, and for making prevail, for carrying from one end of society to another, the best knowledge and best ideas of the time; labouring to divest knowledge of all that is harsh, uncouth, difficult, abstract, professional, exclusive; to humanize it, to make it efficient outside the clique of the cultivated and learned, yet still remaining the best knowledge and thought of the time, and a true source, therefore, of sweetness and light.' This was how he thought Hellenism could be cultivated and spread.

And yet, Arnold is a great poet of loneliness:

> . . . in the sea of life enisled
> We mortal millions live *alone*.

There is a painful tension between what Arnold stood for and what his life was often like. He is a great representative of generous communication and mutual comprehension; he seeks harmony and balance. But he knows isolation, rejection and maddening defeat:

> Creep into thy narrow bed,
> Creep, and let no more be said
> Geese are swans, and swans are geese
> Let them have it how they will.

And so he presents us with a frightening contrast: the cultivation of the best self, beautifully fitted for social life, yet on the road to loneliness. While the ordinary self, which is the cause of feuding and faction, allows one to 'swim with the tide' (as Arnold puts it) in the company at least of a gang of fellow adherents.

Arnold shows us a problem of living: one's best self might be at odds with the society that happens to be at hand. He dignifies this suffering by explaining it: societies tend to reinforce our ordinary selves. But he also sets up an alternative: one in which devotion to the best self is the norm. He desperately wanted to find institutions that would be the worldly homes of this kind of ambition, that would be strong enough to absorb and educate the freedom which political and economic progress had released. He fancied that universities, established churches and government-funded schools could – if reformed – play this role. But he was deeply aware that such institutions – in practice – were often no more than ordinariness armed with prestige and funded by taxations. He imagined a national academy designed to direct and guide the thoughtful life of the nation – carefully pointing out the errors of popular belief, and keeping public attention on the most important issues. Then he imagined a bit more realistically: 'The very same faults which hinder our having an Academy of this kind – the want of sensitiveness of intellectual conscience, disbelief in right reason, dislike of authority – would also hinder us from making our Academy, if we established it, one which would really correct our faults.'

Arnold has put his finger on one of the major difficulties of the world today. We need institutions – churches, newspapers, art movements, universities, political parties – that hold and support the best self; which can express and empower the best self; and which are able to hold their own against the cross-currents of fashion.

7

Pursuing an Ideal

Reflection on the places and sights that seem to show us the essence of civilization supports the view that it has an ideal aspect: civilization is not so much what we have as a picture of what we need. For me, some representative objects of civilization are, to start the list: the classical squares and crescents of the New Town in Edinburgh; a table set for lunch in a quiet, leafy garden; Venice seen across the lagoon; the golden glow of lamplight in a book-ish room, glimpsed through a window walking home at night from the station. What they suggest moves beyond what they actually are: they point to an ideal, even when they fall short in reality.

The New Town has its patches of squalor and dreariness; I've felt crushed by loneliness walking along the elegant streets; many of the locals might be stuffy and cold, as their rivals in Glasgow believe. At lunch one might drink too much and make regrettable comments. The history of Venice includes plenty of bloodshed, intrigue, greed, cruelty, injus-tice, mindless dissipation and pretentiousness. The bookish room might be a place of anxiety and despair, its owner insufferable.

Still, to say that such sights and places, or those on one's own list, are deeply civilized retains its point. Beyond their actual imperfections they seem to tell us of what we really want. The idea is distinct from the reality. None of the meanings currently and commonly assigned to the word 'civilization' seem to quite capture this idea, although they may all have some bearing upon it. The images of civiliz-ation on such a list are connected with material prosperity – but only connected with it. They have something to do with pleasure and satisfaction – but they are also serious and deeply meaningful. They have links with the high achievements of art and culture – but they are also sugges-tive of daily living.

I take from this the thought that we want to – need to – join up intellectual endeavour with the private and intimate questions of life. The question 'What is it to me?' can be asked in a dismissive tone of voice. But when posed seri-ously in the hope of a genuine, revealing and usable answer it lies at the heart of all serious thought.

There is a moment in conversation – and I wish it came more often – when we change gear; it is usually getting late and someone takes a risk. Gradually, intimate trust and relaxation have met; perhaps we have had a few glasses of wine. Much of the time we are conscious of not quite saying what we mean; of not quite being able to say what it is we would say – if only we knew how. Now it is changing. We lean forward: 'Here's how I *really* see life'; 'To be com-pletely honest, this is what I think.' We have cut loose from complaint, from defence, from the clever display of information. Now it's what we love, what we hold dear; what it is like to be you. In pursuit of romance, this would be the moment when flirtation has succeeded: it is no longer a question of teasing and probing while keeping one eye on the exit. We know we do not need the getaway car any more. One life opens to another life.

In the romance of ideas and conversation, this is what we are looking for. It is a kind of revelation; it might take hours to peel away the layers of ordinary niceness: the reasonable reports on what we are up to; the fair descriptions of our official convictions; our gossip about ourselves. One of the candles has burnt out; we listen well, a pause helps, we forget everything except what it is so important to remember: as if we had become the essence of ourselves; as if we had remembered some wonderful secret, and found that the other person remembered it too. A handful of times spread out across the years we might fall into the truest statement of what we are really about.

I am interested in philosophy that can engage with the spirit of such times. This is the promise of the word: a promise not fulfilled in the main ways we think of civilization today. Investigation of any important idea should involve more than intellectual curiosity. When we wonder 'What is love?', 'What is art?' or 'What is the meaning of life?' the hope is that understanding these ideas will provide real insight into the central problems of existence. The promise of civilization is not that we shall grasp an idea; it is that we shall live better, more civilized, lives.

Every so often, I'm struck by a longing to reform the world. It mostly starts with something quite specific: Why is there so much litter in the street? Why are the opinion pages of the newspapers so taken up with arguments that cut across, rather than engage constructively with, each other? Why is yet another depressing building under construction? Why does the government not take more effective action on education, climate change, international conflict?

It is a longing that the world be a more civilized place. And then the idea about what to do in the face of this takes shape: the UN should be reformed; political discourse should be improved; cities should be smaller. For about two minutes the fantasy seems compelling: it is all so simple and clear. Corresponding to this is the fantasy of a book as an instruction manual for a better world.

Against this fantasy comes a sober recognition. It is all too complicated, too difficult; it is not going to happen. Flicking through the newspaper usually does it for me: crime rates, chemical weapons, mortgage stress, war zones, climate change, teenage binge drinking, political corruption – the problems of the world are so overwhelmingly large, complex and urgent.

There is a comment Goethe makes – it is in his *Italian Journey* – which bears on this. He has just been daydreaming about haranguing his fellow countrymen back in Germany and setting them all to rights in his books. But then he remembers the real nature of writing. A book is not actually a set of instructions to some docile executive office that can implement the author's conclusions. Goethe sketches reality: a book will be nibbled by individual readers sitting alone in the corner of a room. This is a powerful, corrective image when thinking about civilization. Because civilization is in some ways such a public concept, so appealingly linked to ideals of social and political significance, it is tempting to proceed as if the task were to draw up an action plan for a perfected United Nations.

My ideal of a book is as an intimate space: it does not particularly point to solutions to the problems of the world or of private life. I do not believe that books are especially good ways of solving those problems. Instead – as I see it – a book is a place where aspects of inner life are at home.

But intimacy and ambition are not as far apart as they

might seem. And I do have a practical agenda, only not one directed at the cabinet office or the White House. It is true that the problems we tend to associate with civilization today are dramatically public: war, poverty, greed, the mismanagement of resources, the erosion of civil liberty, crime, ignorance, depression, pollution, terrorism. All of these can be traced back, eventually, to the most private of places: the inner lives of individuals. The desire to find wisdom and beauty in one's own life need not therefore be a retreat from the task of making civilization: it might be the right place to start.

PART TWO

Civilization as Material Progress

8

The Office and the Spire

My first job, after finishing an undergraduate degree in philosophy, was in the head office of a large insurance company located in the City of London. I often had to research old correspondence connected to difficult claims. The files were stored in a small room on the ninth floor, which no one else ever seemed to enter. It had a single window that, by the misfortunes of urban development, was right next to the spire of one of the churches Sir Christopher Wren designed for the City – following the Great Fire of 1666. The spire was now surrounded and overshadowed. Looking out of the window I had a vision the architect might have dreamed of but which was granted only to pigeons until the insurance company raised its edifice.

Standing on my toes and pressing my forehead against the glass, I could just see the sober and dignified lower part of the church. Seventy-five feet above the level of the street – a couple of floors below me – the square bell tower was transformed into a classical temple: each face a triumphal arch. Level with my line of sight there was a second, slightly smaller, circular temple: a ring of columns around a central core. (I have the plans and elevations before me on my desk and I now realize that this core contains a spiral staircase.)

Above this rose a ring of volutes: great carved scrolls of stone; these support a third and final little octagonal temple: exuberant and airy. Perched on this is an obelisk, at the very tip of which balances a golden ball. Above that, clouds, sky, the endless universe.

This was Wren's solution to one of the great architectural problems of his age: how to use the forms of classical building to construct a spire – the public symbol of an ecclesiastical building, established in the Middle Ages and native to Gothic architecture.

I spent a long time looking out of the window, falling in love with the spire, always listening anxiously for my supervisor coming to find out what was keeping me from my desk.

At the time it seemed to me that there was an unbridge-able chasm between the world of the spire and the world of the insurance company: between spiritual and material prosperity; that my own life was horribly split between these opposed realms. The spire spoke of physical grace, richness of meaning, serenity and seriousness. There was also to my eye a kind of gladness in the building. The sequence of temple forms was the outward show of an inner vitality, confidence and delight in existence: like a dog bounding across a field. The significance of the spire did not seem to me to be purely historical: it was not merely showing me how people used to build. It was a voice in the present speaking of my own needs and aspirations. I wanted those qualities in my life.

By contrast, the insurance company represented an income, security – for me and its clients – and a step in a financially healthy career. Were the office and the spire, and all that they symbolized for me, mutually exclusive? Could I embrace beauty, truth and goodness only by embracing poverty and accepting that the pursuit of these ideals was folly by the economic standards of the world? I was depressed; my situation seemed hopeless.

My dilemma – should I stay or should I go – was resolved for me the day my supervisor finally investigated what was going on in the filing room. He came in quietly, watched me for a few seconds as I gazed out of the window, and told me to clear my desk and never come back.

At the time I experienced this dilemma as a unique curse – although a part of me was proud of my suffering: my pain was special, unshared by others. Other people, I imagined, had little difficulty in standing on one side or the other. My brother was living in a squat in Prague, drinking during the day and playing music in bars in the evening. He had no money but he was free. He had settled for one of the possibilities. On the other side, I imagined my supervisor as completely sure that he was living the right life: doing his work carefully, drawing a good salary, not staring out of the window.

Looking back, I wonder if his annoyance at my behaviour had an additional dimension. Of course, I should have been more diligent. But perhaps he was also warding off his own anxiety by getting rid of me. Perhaps he felt that he could not afford to love the spire or wonder about the meaning of life; he had had to renounce those things. And he enacted on me the humiliation that, he feared, would fall on him were he to admit those longings.

I also came to realize that my brother actually would have liked a more secure existence; he just could not see how that might be possible while he was pursuing creative freedom. It is the ordinariness of this painful split that now strikes me as significant.

9

Efficiency

Towards the end of the eighteenth century Adam Smith supplied a very straightforward answer to the question: What is civilization? In *The Wealth of Nations*, first published in 1776 and still a foundational text, Smith defines a civilized society as one in which there is a high level of productivity and, therefore, a high degree of national wealth.

Smith's career displayed the attractive flexibility of the era: he was Professor of Logic and later held the Chair of Moral Philosophy at the University of Glasgow, he wrote a book about sympathy, made a Grand Tour in the company of a young Scottish duke and then in his forties turned to economics. (He also had the unusual distinction of being kidnapped by Gypsies as a child, although the significance of this experience for his later work has never been precisely defined.)

He starts with a description of an entirely natural society, such as might have been the common human condition for thousands of generations. 'Every individual who is able to work is more or less employed in useful labour, and endeavours to supply, as well as he can, the necessities and conveniences of life, for himself or such of his family or tribe as are either too old, or too young or too infirm to go hunting and fishing. Such nations, however, are so miserably poor that, from mere want, they are frequently reduced to the necessity of directly destroying or sometimes abandoning their infants, their old people, and those afflicted with lingering diseases, to perish with hunger or be devoured by wild beasts.' The point is purely economic. Smith did not despise simple foraging societies or imagine that the lives of such people were without moral dignity and warm human relationships.

What interested Adam Smith was the fact that some modern societies were so much more efficient. 'Among civilized and thriving nations, a great number of people do not labour at all, many of whom consume ten times more than those who work; yet the produce of the whole society is so great that all are often abundantly supplied, and a workman even of the lowest and poorest order, if he is frugal and industrious, may enjoy a greater share of the necessities and conveniences of life than is possible for any savage to acquire.' The total quantity of material provision is much greater, yet the average effort required is much less. In other words, labour is more efficient. *The Wealth of Nations* is largely taken up with tracing the conditions that enable this increase in the quantity of goods produced relative to effort. Smith is – by his own lights – seeking to explain what makes a country civilized.

The key to efficiency and increased production lies in the division of labour. Individuals become more competent at any task through practice. Someone who makes shoes every day will come to make an equivalent article more quickly than another person who combines this occasional task with many others. And the gain will be greater still if the various stages of the process are distributed between different specialists. One person concentrates on getting the hide, another prepares the leather; a third makes the laces; others make the necessary tools. The more civilized, or improved, a society is, the more production becomes specialized and, hence, efficient. Technology is the mechanical version of specialization; in technological progress tools are adapted to more and more specific tasks, and the quantity of human labour required for production drops dramatically.

But specialization cannot take place unless a lot of other developments also occur. For one thing, it depends upon trade. The person who develops an ability to make twenty pairs of shoes in a week has to be making them for other people. The people who make different parts of a single product have to coordinate their efforts. The channelling of energy and ability into particular crafts and subcrafts thus requires the development of markets. More advanced specialization further requires money as a means of exchange. It would be hopelessly complex – and massively inefficient – to maintain the activities of highly specialized workers through barter.

In the course of *The Wealth of Nations*, Adam Smith gradually outlines the complex set of wider, yet interrelated conditions that maximize productivity. These are: the growth and development of towns and cities, which allow large, concentrated markets, which in turn increase the degree of specialization; freedom of trade and freedom of movement of workers, which is important if effort is to be directed where it is most productive; and competition and zealous self-interest, which are engines of economic improvement. Smith was critical of the many monopolies that existed in Europe – while they benefited a few people they were irrational in that they dramatically lessened the overall productivity of societies. The accumulation of private capital is of great importance, because it allows for investment: the creation of specialized industries requires training and outlay before any goods can be sold. So, economic progress depends upon the availability of capital and credit (the reverse situation being fully illustrated in the current global economic downturn). Efficient banking systems and the management of risk requires rational commercial legislation, strictly policed. Civilization progresses as the conditions for increased productivity are met.

If my supervisor at the insurance company had done two surprising things – read Adam Smith and taken an interest in my life – he might have said something like this: 'The building you are in now is a temple to efficiency. What sort of insurance did they have in the seventeenth century? Do you really think life was better then? You'd have been a clerk in a counting house, beaten by your master for staring into space. Almost everyone lived on the edge of poverty, if they hadn't already been carried off by the plague.'

Broadly, all this is true. In so many ways everyday life is much better now than ever before. If it was necessary to choose between the insurance building and all it means and the tower and all the conditions of society that went with it, then you would have to settle for the huge concrete box and the filing room. I am haunted by a question that is both private and public: Under what circumstances could the best of both be attainable? What would allow an individual life or a whole society to have the efficiency of the office and the inspiration of the spire?

A series of questions emerges here. Suppose one looks with a degree of envy upon the sophistication of ancient Athens, and the centrality of drama, architecture, noble athletics, philosophy, oratory and sculpture to their society. Someone will surely point out that the Athenians had slaves and excluded women from public life. The desired thing is put out of reach because its existence seems to depend upon conditions that we cannot accept.

Or consider the construction of Chartres Cathedral. How impressive: a whole society came together for decades, building and rebuilding an incredibly beautiful monument to their hopes and convictions. Can we not do that now? Then the painful facts come to mind: this was a society based on serf labour; in which there was complete agreement about religion – because there was no alternative – little education, no free inquiry; no freedom of conscience. And a great deal of the effort seemed to be occasioned by anxiety about the afterlife.

Think of declines in public civility, in manners and the respect the young should show to the old. In the past, a certain level of public and private good behaviour was maintained by stern demands and expectations. I am amazed, some mornings, when trying to get my children off to school. It takes about twenty minutes of coaxing, pleading and serious diplomacy to get them ready. By the time that is done, I feel I have exhausted my emotional and mental reserves. I know perfectly well that if *my* father had told me to put my shoes on I would have raced to do it. The difference is as simple as it is awkward. I was frightened of disobeying him. I do not think my children are frightened of disobeying me. I am glad they are not, but I do resent the way this complicates even quite minor practical matters. This is a tiny social instance of the same phenomenon: the good things we want seem to slip away from each other. We want both lack of fear and a quick response. It is like the spire: we seem to be faced with a further version of the same dilemma. Either you have a clear social respect founded on fear or you have a greater emphasis upon kindness and a reduction in civility.

Slavery, universal and unquestioning religious faith, aristocratic government, disregard for the suffering of others: these are the very miserable grounds on which some of the major achievements of civilization in the past were built. Hence the thought: we cannot have those desirable things now, because we have got democracy, freedom of conscience, various kinds of equality (nearly), kindness and hygiene instead. If these really are the only options, then we do not have much choice.

The organic conception of civilization reinforces this view. It stresses the interconnectedness of everything that occurs in a particular society in a particular epoch. Therefore the achievements of a time and place are thought of as inescapably bound up with, and often produced by, the defects of the era. If the passage of time sees the removal of those defects it must also remove the possibility of parallel achievements.

According to this view the great public monuments of post-war Britain had to look like Milton Keynes and the Millennium Dome – *because* of democracy and a National Health Service and universal education and freedom of opinion. The seventeenth century could have as its greatest public monuments St Paul's Cathedral and the other churches of Sir Christopher Wren *because* it had oligarchic aristocratic government, poor sanitation, short life expectancy, little freedom of opinion and little public education.

However, we could employ the idea of civilization in a more hopeful way. We could see civilization as seeking to equal the best achievements of the past while disentangling them from the misfortunes upon which they once depended. The idea is that we could aim for the same level of civility, grandeur, grace and beauty, but without building upon those obviously intolerable foundations.

10

Pro and Contra

Adam Smith was the first writer to provide a convincing account of the most advanced economies we have now. But in some important ways he was simply refining a long-standing tradition of thought. The word 'civilization' is of fairly recent origin. It came into regular use in Britain and France only during the eighteenth century; Smith is one of the first writers – perhaps the first who still commands a modern readership – to employ it.

The word derives from the Latin 'civis', which is the root of 'city'. And the connection is revealing about the way civilization was thought of during the Enlightenment. If we were to define 'civilization' as 'city-fication' we would not be completely wrong; although, hopefully, that word will never gain currency.

Here, the big point about civilization is improvement upon the way things just happen to be: it adapts nature to meet human needs. And we can see this in some of the traditional monuments of civilized life. The Pont du Gard – the Roman aqueduct in the south of France and an icon of civilization – carries water high across the valley. It is an artificial river. Instead of running directly to join the Rhône, the waters were made to take a detour through the fountains and baths of Arles. It improves the distribution of water, from the point of view of a human community. In a similar sense, medicine improves health; justice improves outcomes. And it was in this tradition that Adam Smith was working. He took up the broad theme of improvement and explained its workings in a special – and very significant – case: economic efficiency.

Should we adopt Smith's way of thinking? Should we agree that civilization is just the name for the conditions that allow for increased material prosperity? Some of the most compelling sites of civilization – the Grand Canal in Venice, the centre of Paris – are obviously connected to sustained material prosperity. Great material resources were deployed in their creation. At the beginning of the Renaissance, Florence was the richest city in Europe, thanks to its success in banking and the wool trade. Such examples remind us (if we need it) that civilization has an economic foundation.

Smith's idea of civilization is generous to our material needs, desires and ambitions. Rather than castigate us for being too materialistic, he suggests that these longings can be fulfilled. The aspiration to material comfort and security – the desire to own lots of things and hold on to them, to have money and keep it secure – does not often get intellectual support. We are frequently invited to feel awkward and embarrassed about this kind of yearning. But it has very deep roots.

There is an especially revealing example of this desire in the second-last chapter of James Joyce's *Ulysses*. Leopold Bloom, the middle-aged co-hero of the book, is preparing to go to bed. The chapter is structured as a sequence of questions Joyce puts to Bloom. The most interesting is: 'In what ultimate ambition had all concurrent and consecutive ambitions now coalesced?' – in other words, what did this man most want from the world? Here is the answer: '[T]o purchase by private treaty in fee simple a thatched bunga-lowshaped 2 storey dwellinghouse of southerly aspect, sur-mounted by vane and lightning conductor, connected with the earth, with porch covered by parasitic plants (ivy or Virginia creeper), halldoor, olive green, with smart carriage finish and neat doorbrasses, stucco front with gilt tracery at eaves and gable, rising, if possible, upon a gentle emi-nence with agreeable prospect from balcony with stone pillar parapet over unoccupied and unoccupyable inter-jacent pastures . . .'

This is only the beginning of an account that is lovingly extended over several pages, describing the contents, the gardens, the easy access to a train station. There is a great deal of information about the precise economic arrange-ments under which Bloom would purchase this place and meet the running costs. The jargon of law and economics is much used in formulating the answer – but the impulse which is at work in Bloom's imagination is sweetly human. He wants privacy, security and comfort; he wants his fair share of dignity and ease.

Bloom is a universal character. He envisages happiness and a good life in comfort, convenience and material pos-sessions. In his fantasy, there is no mind–body problem. Happiness of mind will be played out through the happi-ness of the body. His dream home fuses material and spiritual longings, drawing them towards the same goal.

The longing for civilization grows out of the dual aspect of human nature. We are physical creatures with minds that aspire to abstract ideals: beauty, goodness and truth. It is this dual nature that compels us to seek two kinds of satisfaction (an income and beauty, in terms of my first job) at the same time. Hence a major source of anguish is the fear that being loyal to one kind of need will force us to neglect the other. The power of Bloom's daydream is that it addresses both types of longing at once.

The pessimistic analysis holds that material and spiritual prosperity are incompatible because the conditions which maximize efficiency in the production of material goods are at odds with human flourishing. The relentless search for innovation; rigorous competition; the unleashing of self-interest: these have produced remarkable material results: billions of mobile phones, CAT scans, hundreds of millions of dishwashers, space probes, thousands of cities, vast oil refineries, the internet, hugely increased farming yields.

But the advancing front of material progress places strains upon individuals. Sometimes this might be expressed in the language of social justice: when market forces deliver immense financial rewards to a few people and very little to many others. Or when the price of success in material terms is the destruction of all other concerns: think of the standard story of the CEO who builds a business from nothing into a global name by making almost inhuman demands on the staff.

Just surviving becomes harder; that is, surviving according to rising expectations of comfort, convenience and reliability. Thus the sources of discontent and frustration grow. The pace of life is more hectic; the demands upon personal resourcefulness are ever increasing. For instance: the vision of what it is to be a good parent has expanded incredibly; the expectation of how long you should be healthy and active, how attractive you should be, how many friends you should have, how much money you should earn. Health, friends, being a good parent: these are all really important. But they can be wrapped up in end-lessly growing demands that we make upon ourselves. One is inclined to feel that 'life is elsewhere': I am not living the life I am supposed to live.

This is a familiar kind of lamentation and it often seems to point to the conclusion that material prosperity is the problem: it is precisely the development of free markets, the expansion of the economy and the mobility of capital that has caused the decline of inner prosperity.

The Tower

Civilization is material prosperity *plus* something else. The character of that something else is to do with inner life: the prosperity of the soul. A prosperity that might be sketched – in its first outlines – as sweetness and light: wisdom and the appreciation of beauty. It is to do with the quality of thought and feeling.

The possibility of integration of these two kinds of prosperity – the marriage of depth and security – is tantalizing. Without material resources, without worldly competence and the ability to wield power, depth of mind and heart is impotent. Virtue becomes a forlorn outcast in the wicked world. It is entirely understandable that sensitive and serious people find themselves identifying with St John the Baptist – crying in the wilderness (or writing books with titles like *Is It Just Me or is Everything Shit?*).

Such a painful split between virtue and success is too old to be blamed on any recent events or conceptual confusions. We can see it in Plato: 'The good man is like one sheltering behind a wall in the hailstorm of life'; and in Christ: 'My kingdom is not of this world'; and in the teaching of the Buddha: 'The good life depends on complete detachment from worldly desires.'

*

Through my childhood, from the age of five to fifteen, my family used to go regularly to Largs: a mildly genteel coastal town on the Firth of Clyde, about forty miles south-east of Glasgow. After a long hotel lunch we would take a walk on the Promenade past a curious structure called the 'Pencil'. It had been erected in 1912 to commemorate a thirteenth-century battle. As a child I thought it was actually an ancient place of refuge, built during the period when Viking raiders pillaged the west coast of Scotland.

The monument has a small doorway set about ten feet or so above the ground. I imagined a few Dark Age locals clambering in, pulling up a rope ladder behind them and sheltering there while hordes of Nordic sailors with horns on their helmets rampaged outside. It was both a reminder of past horrors and a symbol of the normal condition of the world. Civilization was always in there, cramped and cowering. My mother had told me about the retreat of the sixth-century Christian scholars who preserved the last remnants of civilization and saved their skins by withdrawing to craggy islands off the west coast of Ireland. They survived in pitiful flint cells: they were weak, isolated and fearful. My situation, as I saw it then, was essentially the same. Admittedly the deprivations were not quite so extreme: we lived in a hilly suburb – not on the edge of a cliff. I felt not so much that the barbarians were at the gates, but rather that they were pretty much in control of everything, and perhaps always had been.

Everything sensitive and tender and beautiful was frighteningly vulnerable. Goodness was softness; life was hard: only hardness could succeed. It seemed to me not exactly that the good would die young, but something along those lines: the good would not flourish externally, however rich and fine their inner lives might be; and they would have difficulty getting on precisely because they were sensitive, kind and thoughtful.

It is hardly surprising that the two versions of prosperity eye each other with nervous suspicion: there are so many possible points of antagonism. But what we need to understand are the possibilities of integration. We need this because of the tendency in human nature to be devoted to material prosperity. The general cultivation of sweetness and light is going to have to stand alongside, rather than in opposition to, this devotion.

The tower is not only an image of a social problem: barbaric people outside, sensitive people inside. It is also a kind of self-portrait. The delicate part of oneself may be locked away: frightened by one's own barbaric tendencies, and humiliated by the harsh demands of others. Civilization speaks to the individual as well as to whole societies. How can the gracious and tender parts of oneself become potent? This is an intimate problem.

The point, here, is to trace the *connections* between spiritual goods and worldly goods. The thing that sensitive and serious people love (spirit) is already very connected to what they think they hate (matter, materialism). We do not really hate matter and worldly goods, but we can easily feel guilty about our enthusiasm, just as we might feel guilty about sex if we also want to be nice – that is: dignified, kind, sensible. The point of being civilized is that you can be very interested in sex and a good person too; you can be worldly and spiritual. The question is: How?

Return to Adam Smith for a moment. He was discussing material progress in relation to quite basic goods. He was impressed by gains in efficiency, and the consequent lower costs, in the production of bread, cloth, shoes, timber and nails. For people living close to subsistence, as many of his contemporaries were, reducing the cost of producing such goods was a great benefit.

To say that these are basic goods is to say that their use is obvious. We know very clearly why people needed these things and they understood exactly what to do with them, as we do today. But it is precisely this clarity that is lacking when it comes to the other things that tend to bother many people today about consumer goods.

We should take from Adam Smith the core idea that material progress is partly to do with efficiency and reduced costs. Goods are supplied more readily. But what goods are supplied and how they are used cannot be determined merely by considering the process of supply. Demand, and how goods are appreciated and how they are used, depend upon other factors quite different from those Smith draws attention to.

We can sketch another vision of material progress: one in which the quality of demand, and the wisdom of use, increases at the same rate as efficiencies of supply. In that case, material progress would mean a greater, more efficient supply of the things we need for living good lives. In other words, the problem is not material expansion; it is material expansion in the absence of an equal degree of spiritual growth. And it is a mistake to suppose that it is material progress itself that has damaged our spiritual condition.

It is more accurate – and more practically useful – to see the causality running in the opposite direction. It is the weakness of our grasp of spiritual goods – of our attachment to truth, beauty and goodness – that has rendered material progress unsatisfactory in crucial ways. So the proper response is not to set about removing the mechanisms for material prosperity but to concentrate on the task of supporting and diffusing wisdom, kindness and taste.

As I write these three words – wisdom, kindness and taste – I imagine a certain kind of cynical response: these are old-fashioned words, they are evaluative, they are personal, they are elitist, they are conservative. And it is just this response that is at the root of our present difficulty. These are the three qualities that are absolutely essential for the harnessing of material progress to human ends; yet these three qualities have been regarded as illegitimate and irrelevant by many educated people of the second half of the twentieth century.

Materialism looks bad because of a problem occurring elsewhere. Dramatic growth in consumption has happened in the last thirty years: a period when the arts and the humanities have been unambitious in their efforts to guide and educate taste. The accumulated wisdom of humanity, concerning what is beautiful, interesting, fine or serious, was – to a large extent – left to one side at the precise time when the need for guidance was greatest, and when guidance was hardest to give, and so required maximum effort and confidence.

When one looks at celebrated figures of those worlds – such as Andy Warhol or, today, Jeff Koons and Damien Hirst – and asks what does their art say to people about consuming, the answer is very little. I do not want to attack those particular individuals; they seem, among others, to be creations of a profoundly damaged culture that tells itself it is being clever and sophisticated and up to date for the wrong reasons. The cultural laurels – and a species of authority that goes with them – have been awarded in unfortunate directions. Mockery, irony and archness are not what we need.

While the works of these artists have gained amazing commercial success, they suggest a loss of purpose in the arts. Loss, that is, of a really central and powerful claim upon the education of taste: upon the sense of what is beautiful, gracious or attractive.

We have suffered an astonishing corruption of consciousness practised upon us by a decadent cultural elite. Think of the language of contemporay praise: a building is admired because it is 'interesting' – like the average newspaper column. The gap between 'interesting' and 'glorious' or 'adorable' is vast. An artist is praised for being 'provocative' – like someone bleating into a mobile phone on a crowded train. We are miles from 'profound', 'tender', 'magnificent'.

All of this has come about because of a misreading of history. It has been supposed that the point of high culture – of the greatest imaginative and creative effort – is to unseat some fantasized ruling class who had to be provoked and distressed into change. But that is not the task of art or intelligence. Their real task is to shape and direct our longings, to show us what is noble and important. And this is not a task that requires any kind of cagey, elusive obscurity. The way forward here is to be more demanding, truthful and – at first – courageous. We have to forget the shifting patterns of fashion. Something is good because it is good, not because it was created yesterday or five hundred years ago.

12

Flourishing

Raphael's fresco *The School of Athens*, painted in Rome in 1510, depicts the intellectual giants of ancient Greece alongside the great figures of the Renaissance, who considered themselves the descendants of their Greek heroes; including, in a lower corner, Raphael himself. Plato and Aristotle are at the centre, walking together beneath a magnificent series of classical arches. While Plato points upwards to the realm of pure ideas, Aristotle holds out his right hand, gesturing towards the empirical world: the world of touch, vision and experience. In his other hand, he grasps a volume of his own work, the *Nichomachean Ethics*, named after its first editor. It is a study of human flourishing grounded in observation of how people actually live and how things go well or badly. And any ambitious account of civilization has to be an account of how we should live, individually and collectively.

Aristotle's approach to the good life has its roots in biology. Medicine, as the study of individual health, emphasizes the importance of exercise, good diet, keeping away from damp places and out of intense sunlight, getting enough sleep and so on. Such rules have to be adapted to the individual constitution. What will suit an athlete in training for the games at Olympia will not suit a middle-aged merchant. However, it is always possible to recognize excess and deficiency in these areas – even though the lines between them and sufficiency are specific to that person. Someone who happens to need little sleep can still have too little, even by their own limited requirements. Milos the boxer (a favourite example of Aristotle) may thrive on eating large quantities of meat; still, he might overeat, even given the gargantuan quantities appropriate for his physique.

Too little; sufficient; too much: this triad is used again and again in Aristotle's wider investigation of what makes for a good and flourishing life. He looks at the principal areas of feeling and action, and considers how we can be excessive or deficient in any of these fields. Take feelings of honour or dishonour, for instance. Someone may be so taken up with their own honour and self-worth that they become boastful and vain. Another individual may neglect their own honour and be weak-spirited, passive and lacking in a sense of self-worth. Aristotle identifies the middle ground, the 'mean', as he calls it, between excess and deficiency: between taking some part of life too seriously or not seriously enough. In conversation, excess is buffoonery; the deficiency is boorishness, while the best condition is wit – in the old sense of combining mental vitality and engagement.

Aristotle suggests that we are at the same time both musicians and our own musical instruments. Each instrument is – in principle – capable of producing wonderful music. But that depends upon how it is played. Our ability to play is the growth in our capacities, and the music is the exercise of those capacities.

Aristotle tends to assume that there is a fairly close link between flourishing and happiness. However, it is quite important to hang on to one feature of a flourishing life that the term 'happiness' lightly veils. A good life, a wonderful life, is still a life: it is not a fantasy. It must still inevitably have its share of loss, disappointment, suffering, anxiety and self-doubt. These conditions are easily connected to flourishing because they are often inescapable features of doing good things – having relationships; being entrepreneurial or creative; taking responsibility; helping another with a difficult task.

In summary fashion, an updated version of Aristotle's theory of the 'mean' looks like this:

Sphere of action or feeling	Excessive	Mean (or virtue)	Deficient
Fear: how do you deal with danger and with difficulties that make you feel vulnerable?	*Rash*: unwilling to acknowledge real dangers; take risks for trivial reasons	*Courage*: able to confront fairly serious difficulties when there is a good reason to do so; able to tolerate anxiety	*Cowardice*: thwarted by minor fears in pursuit of significant opportunities; tendency to overestimate dangers
Pleasure: how do you have an enjoyable or exciting time?	*Hedonism*: frenzied pursuit of pleasure, leading to desperation and remorse (nothing is ever enough); the pursuit of pleasure endangers other significant goods	*Self-control*: moderation: able to keep the long-term in view; savour and appreciate pleasure; able to break off and come back another day	*Puritanism*: self-denial for trivial reasons; disdain for harmless amusements; displaced anxiety

Sphere of action or feeling	Excessive	Mean (or virtue)	Deficient
Spending money – how much?: are you spending the right amount, relative to what you have?	*Wasteful*: spending more than you can afford; paying more than something is worth	*Liberal*: the best you can afford; able to delay spending; capable of saving	*Miserly*: able, but unwilling, to spend; unkindness disguised as prudence; failure to appreciate quality
Spending money – what on?: given what you have got, are you spending money on the right things?	*Vulgar*: spending a lot, but spending it badly; buying for a bad reason: showing off, peer pressure; too easily led	*Refined*: strong sense of honed purpose; evolving an authentic personal style	*Petty*: lack of imagination; little sense of how money can be spent to enhance life; overimpressed by convention
Self-esteem: how well do you think of yourself?	*Vanity*: blindness to the merits of others; unreal sense of one's abilities	*Sanity*: accurate and stable recognition of ability in comparison with the abilities of others	*Depressive*: tendency to overrate the merits of others relative to one's own capacities
Getting on: how do you advance your own interests?	*Pushy*: irresponsible; wanting more power than you are fit to handle; ungrounded sense of entitlement	*Proper ambition*: determination to make the best use of your abilities	*Unambitious*: inhibited; terror of competition and of failure

Sphere of action or feeling	Excessive	Mean (or virtue)	Deficient
Anger: how annoyed do you get; how often and for what reasons?	*Irascibility*: getting too angry, too often, for too long about too many things; ineffective rage (making things worse by flying off the handle); displaced rage: the fury is really about something else	*Patience*: slow to anger; not afraid to display serious annoyance when there is just cause and when this is the best way of averting a worse consequence	*Lack of spirit*: not getting angry when there is good cause; not getting roused; terrified by the consequences of displaying serious irritation
Social skills: how do you mix with others and present yourself in company?	*Obsequious*: addicted to flattery	*Witty*: bright, to the point, lively; friendly	*Boorish*: lack of interest in conversation, sullen, spoiling
Shame: how do you imagine other people see you?	*Shy*: feeling that one has no right to kindly attention	*Mature*: sane sense of self-worth, but not imposed or intruded; realistic sense of other people's inner lives	*Shamelessness*: no sense that one's conduct may be resented by others with good reason; inability to imagine other people as intelligent but critical

Sphere of action or feeling	Excessive	Mean (or virtue)	Deficient
Indignation: how do you react to the success or failure of others?	*Envy*: feeling humiliated and paralysed by the success of others; denial of the merited success of others	*Reasonable*: dislike it when someone unworthy succeeds just as much as when someone worthy fails; spurred to action by the success of others	*Malicious enjoyment*: delight in the failure of merit

The difference between 'flourishing' and 'happiness' might not seem very great. But the difference in emphasis of these words is significant.

Flourishing is not opposed to happiness; but perhaps 'flourishing' gives a better description of what we actually want than the word 'happiness' does. Happiness suggests a buoyant inner state, a feeling of well-being. But we do not want that in isolation; what we are looking for is satisfaction grounded in character and action. That is why people who are smug – or who are airheads – are so annoying: they seem to enjoy an inner sense of satisfaction that they do not deserve, given their character and actions.

Any deep account of civilization needs to be focused on a vision of human flourishing. Aristotle gives us a very good picture of what individual flourishing looks like. We need to ask about the wider social conditions and arrangements that support and encourage widespread flourishing.

Aristotle invites us to think of things going well in a life primarily in psychological terms. He takes material needs seriously, but what really matters is the condition of mind that they support (for example, security) or which they enable (for instance, generosity). So, we should be looking at the broad social framework that would encourage people to be reasonable, patient, witty, mature, refined, courageous and self-controlled.

This is importantly distinct from the goal of increasing material prosperity; although at times economic growth may support the exercise and development of liberal virtues. This aim is also – less obviously but just as importantly – distinct from the subjective pursuit of happiness.

The pursuit of such a social framework is a very difficult problem for governments, because it is not clear what sort of policy, if any, could induce patience in many people, or make refinement a normal characteristic; what policies would a government introduce if it wished to encourage people to be less envious, or to make vanity less prevalent? What levers to push, how to adjust the tax system to encourage such results?

It is the centrality of flourishing that provides the proper grounds for distance from earlier civilizations and which spurs criticism of one's own and other current civilizations. However impressed one might be by the technical and artistic achievements of the Incas or the ancient Egyptians, one cannot now see these as societies that supported widespread human flourishing. And if we want to question how civilized a modern civilization is, the right question to ask is: How well does it support widespread flourishing?

13

The Hierarchy of Needs

In the 1940s an American psychologist called Abraham
Maslow introduced what he called the 'hierarchy of needs'.
His aim was to organize the apparently chaotic and shifting
realm of human yearning, desire and aspiration. His
method was to categorize 'needs' according to their importance for survival. By this measure, the needs for food,
sleep and water are more basic than the need for shelter;
all of which are more critical to survival than the social
needs of group-belonging and employment. Less urgent
still from the point of view of survival are the needs for
close personal relationships, the winning of the esteem of
others, and the company of others whom one admires.
Least pressing of all are needs for 'self-actualization': that
is, the creative development of a personal style and a mission in life. Those needs that are most removed from the
mechanics of survival are, however, crucial for human
flourishing.

In a reformed, adapted version, the hierarchy looks like
this:

HIGHER NEEDS
Appreciation of beauty
Love of wisdom
Noble sense of purpose
Cultivated imagination
Generosity of spirit
MIDDLE NEEDS
Luxury
Status
Career path
More than enough money
Amusement
Leisure
Social networks
Accurate information
CORE NEEDS
Liberty
Justice
Health (and health care)
Work
Security and a place to live
Literacy and numeracy
Enough money to get by

This hierarchy has a peculiar feature. The higher needs are often modifications of lower (that is, core) needs, and both can attach to the same object. A house provides shelter from the elements, and some degree of physical security: you can lock the doors and keep others out; you can protect your possessions within its walls. But it can also be a primary focus for self-expression and for the pursuit and appreciation of beauty.

Maslow's hierarchy can make it look as if we naturally progress to higher needs when the lower needs are fulfilled. But this is not always the case. Middle needs are perhaps the natural outcome of meeting lower needs, but there is no simple transition from middle to higher needs. And something very strange happens at the top of the hierarchy, for the higher needs have the capacity to absorb and transform the lower needs. So, for example, liberty is valued not only because it is a lot better than oppression – which is what gives it its position as a lower need – but also because it is a precondition for the personal growth that occurs when we recognize and try to meet higher needs.

To many people, middle needs present themselves as the summit of life. So that the acquisition of luxury, the enjoyment of high-status objects and experiences, is taken to be the same as the appreciation of beauty; pursuing a successful career is taken to be the same as having a noble purpose in life.

The battle between middle and higher needs gets a particularly memorable summing-up in a couplet from T. S. Eliot's first great poem, 'The Love Song of J. Alfred Prufrock'. In that poem there is a phrase that gets repeated, as if it is an image that has worried itself into the brain of the poet:

> In the room the women come and go,
> Talking of Michelangelo.

At first glance this might seem pretty unalarming, even rather inviting. Would it not be nice to be in the company of women who enjoyed discussing one of the greatest, most high-minded artists of the Renaissance?

But as we repeat the line something else emerges. The dawdling about of 'come and go' chimes all the way along with 'Michelangelo'. This is not a description of real conversation or real investigation and exchange on a great topic. It is merely polite, almost silly, chatter. The rhyme makes talking about the great artist as empty and directionless as just coming and going – no doubt with elegant posture and perfect coiffeur – at a cocktail party. Here 'civilization' is just veneer. It is the evening's mild entertainment of the leisure class.

This might not constitute a terrible threat to the world: we can live with people chattering about the Renaissance; although it's not a very inspiring image. What is really going on here is that objects which could serve a higher need are being treated as though their function were to satisfy middle needs for small talk.

Civilization depends upon re-imagining middle needs in the light of higher needs. But the intellectual tendency has quite often been in the other direction. Higher needs are dismissed as pompous expressions of middle needs: the appreciation of beauty is just a complex way of demonstrating one's position in the social pecking order; talk of noble purpose is just a way of flattering those who happen to be successful.

One root of this deflationary attitude can be traced to the idea of conspicuous consumption – an idea that became well known through the work of the late nineteenth-century American sociologist Thorstein Veblen.

Veblen has wonderful sport with the idea that much of what we do in life is directed at the task of demonstrating or laying claim to status – and that such status is primarily revealed or claimed through idleness. However, in an intriguing twist idleness gets displayed by consuming the labour, even the idleness, of others. It is a sign of our affluence if we can have a servant: but how much greater is the affluence of the person who can have a servant who does next to nothing: who is largely for display. And the purchase of luxury goods is directed – for the most part – at the display of status. Extending this principle, Veblen argues that learning Latin or Greek was at the time of his writing highly esteemed because it was useless; and learning the correct grammatical forms and the tricky spelling of English words was admired because it displayed the fact that one could devote oneself to useless, even counter-productive, occupations.

Tolstoy gives an extreme example of such display: in *Anna Karenina* he describes the very long fingernails of a high-ranking civil servant; the 'meaning' of the long, manicured nails was just this: 'I am a man who is incapable of doing any manual labour whatever. I cannot even do up a button or tie a shoelace. But, as you see, I am perfectly dressed.' Hence: 'I have others to do everything for me.'

Veblen imagines a society preoccupied with conspicuous consumption, where the quest is not 'What is good about what I am doing?' but rather 'How can I lay claim to high standing by being wasteful?'

This point has not merely been well taken, it has become a commonplace: it is routine to hear the great arts of the past explained in terms of the display of status. In short, there is a deflationary analysis of 'higher things' lingering in the wings here and eager to take centre stage. So-called higher things are just those that maximize conspicuous consumption.

But there is a problem at the heart of this analysis, which Veblen partly acknowledges. And that concerns the identification of what kind of consumption will actually display status. One might – for example – try eating ortolans wrapped up in large bank notes, as a character in Disraeli's novel *The Young Duke* is said to do. But the accusation – in that novel – is not mingled with awe or respect. On the contrary, the anecdote is intended to show how disgusting and stupid the character is. In other words, the mere display of wealth (roasting bank bills) does not in itself entice admiration. Veblen concedes this point and notes that the practices and objects of conspicuous consumption need to have some anchor in our evaluative scheme other than the mere fact that they cost a lot of money to procure.

A major thrust of the civilizing process is to develop people's appreciation: to move them from attachment to secondary characteristics of goodness, namely: status and price, to attachment to primary characteristics: beauty and reason. This involves enhancing the quality of the relationships people have to the things they admire. The move is from satisfaction in how others might see one to an appreciation of what is good.

This is a move from a middle satisfaction to a higher satisfaction. It raises the dignity of the individual. The development is revealed by the true answer to the question: What is it about you that leads you to revere or like this thing? In a middle satisfaction, the true answer is: 'I am reassured by the fact that others admire this thing: the object or idea answers my need for social reassurance.' In a higher satisfaction, the true answer is: 'I admire this object; it meets my understanding of what is good.'

Aristotle discusses three kinds of interpersonal bond: comradeship, collaboration and true friendship (which stand in an ascending hierarchy of quality): each kind of bond is related to what you are attending to in the other, and to what is alive within yourself in the relationship.

There are people in whom you can see everything – because you put it there; or others in whom you can see nothing – because you cannot find it. The quality of a relationship depends upon what we can find in the other, which depends partly on what there is to find; and also partly on what we can mobilize in ourselves, which in turn depends on what is in ourselves there to mobilize.

In other words, when we develop a sense of our own capacity for loving we become simultaneously more generous and also more demanding. This is the essence of taste; it is not just another name for personal preference; it identifies a special capacity in the formation of preference. It is the pursuit of a high quality of relationship that feeds discrimination; it is the sense of what in you needs to be met that encourages and drives the longing to discover its proper object in the world. And much of what we tell ourselves about the reasons why we ought to admire something do not hit the target at all; they do not engage with the real sources of longing in oneself for primary goods, but are instead distorted through a well-meaning but in the end mistaken attachment to secondary signs of goodness.

The link between material and spiritual prosperity is made through desire. For what people want – and how much they want it – is a reflection of their inner condition; and it is also the driving force of the world economy. Consumerism – as description of commercial enterprise – is the devotion of businesses to discovering what people want and then targeting those desires more accurately and meeting them more efficiently than their competitors. Today, advertising is not so much directed at stimulating new desires (converting people to appetites they might not have had before – which was the old model) as to alerting potential customers and clients to how well a particular product or service meets their existing desires. Thus the essential advertisement today is a presentation of a consumer saying: 'I am an expert in what I want.'

This vision is intended to be morally neutral: any desire, within the law, is of equal standing. Questions are asked only about the supposedly rational and expert consumer's strength of preference – expressed as an economic opportunity cost. What are you willing to forgo in order to have this thing? How much are you prepared to pay? How much do you want it?

This stance is not interested in the larger meaning of a desire. It pays no attention to the fact that desires are precipitates – expressions – of the individual's degree of spiritual prosperity. To pick up on earlier discussions: a desire is a thesis about flourishing. A seven-year-old who wants to work in an ice-cream van when they are grown up is making a guess, expressed as a desire, about what a good life might involve and what its details might be like. And a great many of our desires have this character.

On hearing about the ice-cream career, adults smile because they know that with further experience, self-knowledge and maturity the picture of a good life will undergo dramatic revision. Fourteen years later the hypothesis of a flourishing life will be reoriented to investment banking, film-making or public charity work – as restatements (although not necessarily more accurate) of a thesis about what a good life for this person would be. The central question is the adequacy of the hypothesis. The desire is answerable to the future.

*

The consequences of a free-market economy are dictated in large part by the quality of desire multiplied by affluence. If the quality of desire is less than zero – that is, if it is an obstacle to flourishing – then the higher the affluence the worse the world becomes. If the quality of desire is high then the greater the affluence the better: since affluence arms desire. The better the desire, the more we should want affluence. This cannot be captured in a morally neutral account of desire.

This all coheres with taking flourishing rather than happiness as the proper goal of life. It may well be the case that happiness flattens out as affluence rises. Extra money cannot, beyond a certain point, purchase much more subjective well-being. But there is no reason why flourishing should flatten out – because it is not structured like an appetite, but rather like a building (or the growth of a tree).

Quality of desire – which is the relationship between wanting and flourishing – is a central issue for civilization. For example: in Jarred Diamond's recent book *Collapse: How Societies Choose to Fail or Succeed* there is a poignant description of the demise of early Danish settlements on the western coast of Greenland. As he reports it, the Danish settlers had before them – in the technology, habits and techniques of the natives – all that they needed to acquire in order to flourish in that difficult region; but they wanted to remain in the tradition of Denmark and to enact the kind of farming and fishing they already knew about; their desire was therefore at odds with flourishing.

The core problem of Western civilization is that material prosperity has increased rapidly while spiritual prosperity has not increased to the same extent. What this means is that there is a general disproportion between the material wealth of the West and its capacity to use that wealth for self-actualization.

This issue has made some impression on commercial thinking. Consider the company mission statement of a leading pharmaceuticals business: 'We will provide branded products and services of superior quality and value that improve the lives of the world's consumers.' Hold on to the grandeur of the ambition: 'improve the lives of the world's consumers'. As yet, the improvement is focused only on basic needs. The major rival of this company is equally noble in its stated aim of adding 'Vitality to Life . . . helping people look good, feel good and get more out of life.' (Slightly worrying that 'Vitality' has a capital letter – as if it might be a supplement, something you drink or eat, rather than a pervasive quality of being.) Google's mission is: 'to organize the world's information and make it universally accessible and useful'. Hegel shared this mission: the grandest possible intellectual project.

The loftiest purposes are often alluded to in advertising, although the products in question tend to come as an anticlimax: 'You gotta have soul' – so buy a mobile phone; 'It's cool to be intelligent' – so install a drinks dispenser.

If you were cynical you could view these messages as deceptions – as ridiculous fabrications. They could be seen as sinister seductions, in which the seducer knows that pretending to be nice is the only way to succeed, but has no real commitment to any of the things they are saying: 'You have such beautiful eyes' is the flattery it takes – but the intent behind the words is entirely self-interested.

But perhaps we should look at these claims in a more generous light: what they suggest are very interesting ambitions – and also (I believe) recognition of a deep problem and a deep opportunity. These are statements about real human motivations: What do I want to do with my life? In this company: What do we as senior strategists employing many thousands of people actually hope to accomplish (alongside making money)? The problem here is not one of cynicism: it is the gap between a genuine, good intent, and the delivery.

The background assumption is that people are trying to do something both vague and noble in their lives: have soul (be interesting, have nice friends, be full of beans), be intelligent yet on top of things, a little bit deep and yet approachable and fun. These are very good things to want. The problem is the gap between the aspiration and the products on offer, which do not have the remotest chance of actually furthering those dreams of self-realization. The future of business – and perhaps of civilization – depends upon raising the product to the level of the hope.

14

Integration

In *A Room of One's Own* Virginia Woolf describes a day she spent at Cambridge; in her account she contrasts a lunch and a dinner.

The lunch was especially pleasing: she tenderly records the luxurious dishes and wines. But what really matters is the effect this has upon her, as she eats and drinks, and sinks back into elegant comfort: 'by degrees was lit, half-way down the spine, which is the seat of the soul, not that hard little electric light which we call brilliance, as it pops in and out upon our lips, but the more profound, subtle and subterranean glow which is the rich yellow flame of rational intercourse. No need to hurry. No need to sparkle. No need to be anybody but oneself. We are all going to heaven and Vandyck is of the company – in other words, how good life seemed, how sweet its rewards, how trivial this grudge or that grievance, how admirable friendship and the society of one's kind.'

Dinner by comparison was mean and depressing. Everything about it speaks of penny-pinching and making do. After the dreary main course: 'prunes and custard followed. And if anyone complains that prunes, even when mitigated by custard, are an uncharitable vegetable (fruit they are not), stringy as a miser's heart and exuding a fluid such as might run in misers' veins who have denied themselves wine and warmth for eighty years and yet not given to the poor, he should reflect that there are people whose charity embraces even the prune. Biscuits and cheese came next, and here the water-jug was liberally passed round, for it is the nature of biscuits to be dry, and these were biscuits to the core. That was all. The meal was over. Everybody scraped their chairs back; the swing-doors swung violently to and fro; soon the hall was emptied of every sign of food and made ready no doubt for breakfast next morning.'

The first meal is inspiring – the second dispiriting. And a big factor in the difference is obviously money. Woolf is pursuing the justification of luxury – because of the broadening of the spirit and the appetite for life that comes with it: the generosity and elegance of mind that it encourages. She presents the awkward evidence that spiritual prosperity might stand on the shoulders of material prosperity. The point is not just that material deprivation saps the energies of the mind. Woolf suggests a more intimate and more productive relationship: the fine deployment of material resources does something more than release us for other concerns; the fish and the wine, the room and the atmosphere create the conditions in which the spirit can expand.

Virginia Woolf is not asserting the false claim that luxury automatically generates nobility of mind; far from it. Her essay raises the stakes: it is a call for luxury to justify itself. Hers is a truth that has few friends. Those fond of luxury will not like the implication that *mostly* it does nothing for inner life. Those devoted to spiritual prosperity – for the most part, less than wealthy – do not like the idea that the flowering of the mind *can* be importantly connected to expensive pleasures.

Woolf is showing us one point where material and spiritual prosperity play up to one another. They do not merely coexist. Each transforms the other. Under the sway of spiritual prosperity, material resources become gracious and dignified. Under the influence of material prosperity, spiritual longing grows warm and generous. Cynical reflection (which is very understandable, since prompted by the most normal of vices: envy) sees only mutual corruption: comfort makes thought merely the defender of privilege; intellectual duty points only towards bleak austerity.

Like Virginia Woolf, I am trying to identify the sweet spot where the two kinds of prosperity intersect and enhance one another. In my private imaginative repertoire, this ideal homes in on a single street in Edinburgh, located just to the west of the New Town. It was developed in the 1820s by the portrait painter Henry Raeburn and named after his wife. Ann Street is composed of two rows of fairly modest, fairly plain, mostly two-storey terrace houses facing each other across long front gardens that lead to the central roadway. This is not one of the grander streets in the city, but it is representative: it captures, in a small compass, many of the ideals of urban planning upon which the city's architectural reputation is based. When we stroll up and down this street (actually or in imagination) the wider implications of the idea of civilization start to become apparent.

Fortunately, Ann Street is not much of a thoroughfare: it comes out at one end near a romantic little gorge, with small cliffs and a tumbling stream. There is little traffic: the narrow road does not sever the gardens. The central blocks of the long terraces on each side step forward slightly; and they have a rather more dignified air: there is a hint of grandeur in the classical pediments that rise above them. At each end a larger block juts out towards the road so that the whole place has an enclosed quality. It is as beautiful as a small street can be.

Why does a place like Ann Street speak profoundly to us? If we take it as a representative 'moment' of civilization, what is the deeper lesson? What is it telling us about civilization? The core point is that the street is desirable. It is attractive and appealing. I am not saying that there should be lots of streets that look exactly like this one – although it is not such a bad idea. But we want a lot more streets that are as appealing. It is a reminder that civilization is connected to happiness and the flourishing of individual lives.

The street is founded upon worldly resources and practical competence; but it harnesses these to something else: a compellingly attractive vision of life.

A place like Ann Street is a macrocosm: a larger version of our own lives, in which we see individual, private hopes accomplished on public scale. Think of the broader background: for much of the eighteenth century Scotland was a backwater, a rather impoverished, damp country on the edge of the world. It suffered internal divisions and external competition. Yet from this apparently unpromising situation it was possible to produce an exceptionally fine new town and then – as a condensed expression of this achievement – a street like the one we have been looking at.

Here we see, also, the transformation of lower needs by the cultivation of higher concerns. It has to be admitted that Ann Street is concerned about status, about community security, about shelter from the elements and about material conveniences. But status, here, is founded upon something very fine – respect is sought on the basis of the real merits of the street. It actually is gracious and dignified, and appreciation of those qualities rightly grounds some measure of respect for the people who choose to live there: because their choice seems to be (and very probably is) a demonstration not so much of their monetary prowess as of their sensitivity, wisdom and taste.

Essentially, civilized life is to do with the integration, the mutual enhancement, of these two kinds of prosperity: material and spiritual. And I think this is why the ideas of civilization and civilized life are so important to us. They name a kind of integration that many people actually do seek, without – perhaps – quite recognizing what it is they are longing for.

At present, this longed-for integration is hard to achieve. The history of civilization is, in one important aspect, the history of the achievement and loss of integration. Sometimes the material competence, the organizing powers and resources of a civilization are much less developed than their spiritual ambitions. The longing for meaning and the imaginative demands of people lose contact with the pragmatic business of individual and social life. A society that is spiritually rich but materially chaotic is no longer a thriving civilization. But nor is one that is materially prosperous but spiritually in decline.

PART THREE

Civilization as the Art of Living

15

The Crooked Timbers of Humanity

An account of civilization is a view about human flourishing. But if flourishing is to be more than an unattainable ideal, we have to see civilization as a realistic project: that is, as grounded in an understanding not only of the appealing possibilities of life, but also of the difficulties of existence.

In 1516 Sir Thomas More wrote a short book that has had a long life; it brought to popular attention a name now linked to an entire genre of writing and a whole way of thinking and feeling: *Utopia*. More had a spectacularly successful career, becoming Lord Chancellor, until he was imprisoned – and finally beheaded – because he refused to acknowledge Henry VIII as head of the Church of England.

It is shockingly easy to imagine societies that are finer, more enticing and lovelier than any that have existed upon earth. Often these have been frankly fantastical: stories of a land where the rivers run with wine and pheasants fall ready-roasted from the sky. By contrast, More's *Utopia* is an attempt to explain in some detail how a society could overcome what he sees as the basic problems of human nature, and to describe how such a society might actually work.

His perfect society is located on a large island, shaped

like a crescent. The pointed ends almost touch and they embrace a vast, tranquil inner sea. By great good fortune, the island is impregnable: the outer coasts are all jagged rocks and precipices and the opening to the inner sea is so narrow that it is easily guarded.

More takes the plausible view that people are by nature quite possessive. We want our own things – private property – and we want to keep them for ourselves. He also sees that this is the cause of a great deal of human misery. If there were no private property there could be no theft, no hoarding, no avarice, no lawsuits, no struggles over inheritance.

So, elaborate laws and arrangements are put in place to guarantee plenty of everything needful even though there is no individual ownership of anything. Everyone is required to live in the same sort of house; all towns are to be similar; everyone spends some time working on the land and some time following a useful trade. Everyone has to change houses every five years, to prevent a sense of ownership growing gradually through long occupation. This emphasis upon similarity is intended to overcome vanity and concern with status. There is not much to be vain about and little to indicate status. The leaders of the society do not have more pleasant or exciting lives than their fellows.

More provides clear proposals linking problems of life (greed, vanity, status seeking) and imagined solutions (equality, universal plainness, agrarian communism). He is exploring the idea that the defects of human character can be weeded out by good government. The task of government is not merely to keep at bay the worst excesses of desire. The aim is not to limit damage, as police forces, law courts and prisons seek to do, but rather to remove the source of the problem. More's political ambition is to lead people to a condition of existence in which the roots of possessiveness and status seeking have been pulled up.

Even if, in some moods, this sounds appealing, it is hard to see how any existing society could become like Utopia. There is no path from here to there. How does More imagine this ideal society coming into being? He explains how the island was conquered and then reorganized by a supremely benevolent dictator. This is too much good fortune: that a single individual would be a brilliant general, an exceptionally wise and far-sighted legislator, yet devoid of any self-seeking or hope for personal gain or glory.

The evident weakness of this practical proposal is reflected in the name of the book. The word 'utopia' is a scholarly pun; in fact, it is a depressing thesis compressed into a single word. Literally, 'utopia' means 'no place'. The 'u' comes from the Greek prefix meaning 'not'. However, when spoken in English it sounds the same as 'eu' – another Greek prefix that indicates something good, as in 'euphoria' and 'eulogy'. The good place, the perfect society, is also a nowhere land.

And, in any case, the plain, regimented, static society that More describes does not sound very civilized. The price of removing human folly seems to be to remove everything that makes life fascinating, beautiful and meaningful. It is a world where there are no splendid buildings, no dramatic ambitions, no powerful clashes of opinion. Nor would there be much space for elegance, romance, cultivated individualism or artistic expression.

A critique of More's ideas was put forward by his close friend Erasmus in a provocatively titled little book: *In*

Praise of Folly. (The folly book actually came out before *Utopia*. But Erasmus wrote most of his 'praise' at More's house, and it is entirely probable that More, who was a great conversationalist, was talking about his ideas for a good society long before he published his own book.) The original title, *Moriae Encomium*, uses the Greek word for 'stupidity', 'moros' – hence our crudely abusive term 'moronic'. It was just too temptingly close to the name of his learned, wise and very dear friend. Erasmus makes his general point like this: 'Without me' – says Folly – 'the world cannot exist for a moment.'

By 'folly' Erasmus means much more than the occasional silly mistake. 'Folly' covers a wide range of behaviour. Vanity, for example, is a species of folly. Vanity involves thinking rather better of oneself than is reasonable. Hence the vain person often expects undue admiration: 'Don't you just love my car, hat, dog, face . . . ?' Folly, or foolishness, is evident when people attach weight to status and all the little markers of social respect. We are foolish when we get carried away by passion; when we go in for wishful thinking; when we blame others for matters that are our own responsibility; when we exaggerate or deceive ourselves. We might admit we are foolish when we live at all.

It goes without saying that 'folly' messes up life: it is destructive. It is the source of so much that goes wrong for oneself, for others, for societies. It is entirely understandable that social reformers should wish to rid the world of 'folly' and should seek to safeguard us against ourselves.

Erasmus calls his book a 'praise' of folly; this is meant ironically. He does not like folly. But as he multiplies the examples of human stupidity, greed, corruption and confusion, something else begins to emerge: the sheer normality of messing things up. Erasmus is no longer castigating an aberration, which – with a bit of coaxing and prodding – could be put right. He seems to be describing our fate.

If we take this seriously, the pursuit of civilization cannot be cast as the project of removing folly from the world. It has to aim lower: at coping and trying to flourish, given the crooked timbers of humanity.

One example of the ineradicable character of folly is that we suffer the weakness of our strengths. The intense devotion that allows us to do certain things well becomes an encumbrance in other areas of life. The person whose profound hatred of injustice makes them an admirable social reformer might also be tiresome as a social companion and nightmarish as a parent. Henry James invented the phrase 'weakness of strength' to describe his Parisian acquaintance, the Russian writer Turgenev. The indecisive, unhurried nature of Turgenev's art was replicated in his inability to keep appointments while being equally unable to decline invitations.

What this indicates is that it would be impossible to correct the annoying habit without endangering the admired talent. Of course this is a rather easy example, because being late is not so very awful and because the novels are really rather good. The credit comfortably outweighs the debt.

What about a more painful example from closer to home? I am drawn to X, an old friend, by his intense and dramatic sense of the complexity of life. He is the sort of person with whom, after fifteen seconds, one is grappling with the hardest issues of existence. He is extremely demanding of me: Am I shying away from the real issue? Am I failing to admit what is really going on? Can't I be more honest, more truthful, more upset, more joyous? It is exhilarating and a bit frightening. His devotion to integrity and knowledge is glorious, but this virtue has made his life hard. It puts a great strain on relationships. It makes the normal compromises of employment difficult. One would not cut away (supposing it were possible) the qualities that make him an enthralling companion and a heroic individual; yet in other ways these are weaknesses.

Such examples can be easily multiplied. Of the people I know reasonably well, I am not sure if there is even one whose strengths are not also weaknesses. Their merits and the price they have to pay for these elsewhere in life seem woven together.

16

The Beast in Me

The idea that there is a 'beast in me' – that human nature is grounded in a set of demands and tendencies that have no connection with, and no loyalty to, refined morality – is explored in Thomas Mann's magnificent novella *Death in Venice*. The central character, von Aschenbach, is on holiday at the Lido. He has lived a life of exemplary devotion to noble values – he has worked extremely hard and achieved great success as a literary artist of the highest standing. But now, well into middle age, he is overwhelmed by the experience of love; he meditates on the most refined idea of erotic desire. He thinks of the Platonic ideal of the desire for beauty leading the lover towards a vision of perfect and comprehensive truth. But in his sleep von Aschenbach is assailed by the other side of love: lust. He dreams of the orgiastic, sadistic rites of Bacchus, in which every kind of sensual excess is desperately pursued, in which his personality seems to fall apart in a violent, ecstatic transgression of civilized values.

A first reaction might be to think that Aschenbach's ideal vision, his cultivated idealism, is now revealed as a sham. It was just a screen for – a deceptive denial of – his real and very dirty nature. But something much more interesting is going on. For, within the narrative, within the story, there is no shying away from this part of Aschenbach's personality. Within this immensely civilized short story, the inflamed destructive imagination is allowed its place; it does not have to be shut up in a cage. At the same time it is not seen as somehow more real than anything else about Aschenbach.

When I was seventeen I spent the early summer in the south of France with my father. Driving back to Glasgow we stopped for a couple of days in Paris. My father was keen to visit the Delacroix Museum and suggested I came along. In principle I rather wanted to; but I'd been nurturing another plan. I told him – and it was not entirely untrue – that I preferred Claude and Poussin to Delacroix. I would go to the Louvre and meet up with him for lunch. As soon as I was on my own I headed for the red-light district and squandered my holiday money in a hot little attic room, pursuing an erotic scenario that had recently gripped my imagination.

Afterwards, descending the exceedingly shabby staircase, I felt a terrifying inundation of self-disgust. I was wicked, stupid, naive, vile, corrupt, irresponsible, thick, wasteful, out of control, nasty, brutish. As I wandered miserably towards the square where I was to meet my father I passed a bookshop. The peaceful, old volumes, which I would have loved to have owned, were now reproaches: my cash had all been consumed. I could have had one of these books; it would have been a joy for ever; in future years it would have been a memento of a lovely morning; I would have taken possession of its wisdom; in some imagined future I would take it down carefully from the shelf and turn its pages with a happy sense of the continuity of life.

But I had destroyed all that. I had chosen instead half an hour of what now seemed like pointless squalor. The evident boredom of the woman I had been with was a painful token of our lack of intimacy. My pathetic attempts to make her grasp some particular action I wanted her to perform, the specific desires I wanted her to satisfy, were now my primary memories. This was what I had locked inside myself.

A little further on I passed the front of a small church. A choir was rehearsing: their voices could just be heard in the street. I looked in; it was a scene of remarkable serenity and patient effort; the conductor was taking them through a limpid, simple – and astonishingly beautiful – piece by Fauré. The mild and tender line of the music felt like an invitation: you must be like me; then you will be happy. It seemed completely real and agonizingly far away. The music expressed what I wanted now; only it was too late; I had cut myself off. Standing in the porch of the church, listening as the conductor rapped his baton cleanly on the back of a chair and they sang again, I started to cry.

At lunch my father told me all about Delacroix, and I lied a little about the Louvre, enough to signal that it would be embarrassing to ask me how I had actually spent the morning. As I ate my omelette and sipped my glass of beer I wondered idly if there was a new story I could spin to get my father to give me some cash and leave me free for the afternoon and whether I would be able to find again the door that led up to the tiny, sordid chamber.

This episode was, for me, unusual only in its dramatic neatness: the deception, the spending of money, the scene at the church door. Thematically it was all too familiar. It all seemed like an endless struggle between sex and civilization. My troubles, I felt, originated in the fact that I was not civilized enough. If only I loved, or understood, Fauré or Delacroix or the pictures in the Louvre more and better, then I would no longer experience the urges that took me away from them.

My guiding image was to be found in an opera by the eighteenth-century German composer Gluck. In *Orpheo* the hero has to rescue his wife, Eurydice, from Hades. But to reach her he has to get past Cerberus – the triple-headed dog-monster who guards the entrance to the Under-world. Orpheus is, however, the first great musician, and as he plays a noble, delicate theme on his lyre, the insistent growling of the beast is lulled; Cerberus is pacified, Orpheus can pass on and the redemptive work of love can proceed.

Cerberus was sex-me and Orpheus was civilized-me. If the civilized part could become strong enough then it would quieten the beast. If only I could be civilized enough I could become a good and wholesome person.

What does this episode say about civilization? The mistake I made was to think of civilization as the attempt to eradi-cate the 'beast in me'. In this guise, the watchwords of civilization are self-control, purity and dignity. A better conception of civilized life would not mock those terms, but it would see that they are asking too much. Instead, a wiser vision of civilization would give equal weight to coping with the tensions between ideals and reality. Its language would be enriched by tact, compassion, privacy and diplomacy. These terms hold on to both sides of the equation: they are interested in what is going on in the little room *and* in what is happening at the church door.

There is something here that we might easily overlook. Compassion and tolerance are civilized virtues only when they also keep one eye on noble ideals. The crucial distinction is between an attitude of indulgence – 'it doesn't matter what you do' – which robs the church-door experience of its dignity and depth; and the accommodation of folly, which keeps faith with ideals, but knows how difficult they are to maintain.

In Rome in 1807, Ingres painted a portrait of Madame Devauçay. In this remarkable picture we contemplate not merely the appearance of a particular woman, as she was in Rome in 1807; this is, almost, the face of civilization itself.

What can be seen in her face? Her gaze – as she looks at us – is steady and clear, uniting inner poise and alert attention to the world. She is at ease with her body: alive to sensuous charm yet not preoccupied or vain; she will listen and understand yet speak with the authentic voice of her own mind. Her hovering smile is a visual translation of that of the *Mona Lisa*; but she has left the realm of mystery; she is a creature of this world, our world: she is fully, wonderfully human, and her humanity is not a burden: she is happy.

This picture is important – at least to me – because it portrays an aspect of civilization that I need in my own life. If I could have taken my sexual troubles, and their present-day counterparts, to her I would have found the right kind of help. I imagine that she would understand, she would be interested and sympathetic. She appears to be able to hold together elegance and erotic complexity; the parts of her that know about the little room do not have to abandon the parts of her that know about noble art and music. She is a counter-instance to the understandable worry that civilization is a cold ideal; that it frowns upon our weaknesses and looks down on dirt and folly. (Perhaps to many people this will seem a minor matter or a simple point. But in my life it has been extremely difficult.)

How is this integration and generosity achieved? In her mind the primary concern is living a good life: human flourishing. It is this purpose that makes sense of prohibitions and ideals of respectability. She understands privacy and discretion; a secret is safe with her. But she does not mock what is secret; she does not think that privacy is hypocrisy. She finds her way carefully between the demands of inner and outer life.

17

Responding to the Human Condition

Two foundational myths have had a profound influence on the way civilization has been conceived. In the seventeenth century the English philosopher Thomas Hobbes sought to describe the condition of life – as he imagined it – that prevailed in the early stages of historical human development. In this 'state of nature' each adult person is more or less as powerful as everyone else. Although, of course, there are variations in physical strength, these are of limited significance. Even a weakling can pick up a stone and creep up on a stronger enemy in the dead of night. This is the war of all against all, a situation in which there is no possibility of undertaking any long-term venture: for whatever an individual produces will be stolen by another. Life is 'nasty, brutish and short'.

The way out of this predicament is through subordination: everyone bows down before a single lord – freedom is renounced for the sake of security. Civilization is seen as a rigorous artifice, designed to save us from ourselves. Life is regarded as a mess that needs to be cleaned up. We need to subordinate our wayward desires to law or rationality or justice: ideals that carry a prohibition, that deny our wishes.

The other myth describes the state of nature in the

opposite terms: at first all was well; each person lived in friendship and harmony with others, the bounty of nature easily met the simple and wholesome wants of all people. Life was sweet and satisfying. But by some misfortune a few people took precedence over others, sought to accumulate greater provisions, and forced the rest into servitude. The way out from this is to return to nature: simple wants and non-possessive attitudes. Civilization destroys and denatures life.

These stories set themselves up in opposition. But what if each is telling us something important? This was what Sigmund Freud thought. The significance of these stories, he held, has nothing to do with historical fact; it lies in the way they present contrasting states of mind, which are then projected backwards and restated as claims about the external world. And, Freud asserted, far from being exclusive claims, each expresses a normal and important state of mind. He saw them both as powerful fantasies that normally coexist in a single person's inner, perhaps unconscious, life.

The first fantasy is of violent conflict, leading to violent subordination, control and domination, where one person enslaves the world. The second fantasy is of concord and universal love, in which everyone is friends with and helps everyone else. In *Civilization and Its Discontents* (1930) Freud argued that normal human relationships exhibited both of these characteristics: in the core, representative relationship we seek both control and free love.

Thus there occurs a type of experience that is of central importance for civilization: the recognition of the tension between these two primary longings. We know ourselves as capable of and as seeking violent dominion over the people we love, which is also to destroy them and therefore lose their love. This generates an internal prohibition – a conscience, or judgement upon ourselves. Freud termed this the 'over-I', rendered more mysterious by the English use of the Latin phrase 'super-ego'.

This means that we internalize the restraints which allow the preservation of loving connections to other people; but at a price: we have to do violence to ourselves and this makes us sad. We have to feel guilty about urges from which we cannot escape. The 'death instinct', or destructive urge – the urge to renounce the claim of others, to do away with their demands or needs – never really goes away.

Thus Freud came to the view that civilization is necessarily a source of human 'discomfort', and that the notion that we can shrug off this discomfort by being more natural, by removing the sense of guilt or shame, is an illusion; albeit one that is likely to persist.

A FEELING FOR TRAGEDY

From time to time life forces its horrors upon us; and in one crucial capacity, the promise of civilization has been to reduce our vulnerability to what used to be called fate. We have taken up arms against misfortune – with mixed success – under the banners of preventative medicine, health-and-safety regulations, insurance companies, divorce courts, relationship counselling. But none of this can remove the deepest intimate horrors: the disasters to those we love, which we shudder from naming even in the privacy of our own heads.

The tragic sense of life has its origin in our determination to carry off two incompatible, but equally serious, ambitions: to search for meaning and to face reality. An intense, unceasing demand for meaning – the longing for life to make benevolent, beautiful sense – is coupled with the dawning, appalling fact that it does not, in the end, make sense in that way. Tragedy is the name for horror seen against the backdrop of love.

This is an area in which civilization does not reduce our suffering – does not make life more pleasing or comfortable. What is the achievement of tragedy? It is to present the deepest sorrows of the human condition: what we love is terribly vulnerable; each life is a brief, scarring moment in the wastes of eternity; our transient existence will be marked by depression, confusion and fear. 'In headaches and in worry/ Vaguely life leaks away.' The ambition of tragedy is to hold such intelligent fears in a ceremonial act endowed with splendour and grace. The ceremony does not overcome our fears. But, unlike horror, it does not seek to stoke anxiety. The tragic view is, really, a determination to hold on to nobility, love and beauty – even while knowing the worst about ourselves.

In an intimate way, tragedy is founded on the fact that not all good things are compatible: it may be (for most people) impossible to have a happy marriage and a raucous erotic life; or to have a well-paid job and follow your own vocation; it may be that you cannot live in the place where you most want to live; responsibility is tedious and frightening; yet taking responsibility is important. The longing to live an interesting and enjoyable life is always confronted by poverty, fragility, bad luck, death. Things we want to control are often beyond our control. We do not choose the political, moral or economic world in which we have to live; you can wear yourself out seeking genuine progress and end up making none.

So the ambition of civilization, in the face of this, is to

strengthen us to face inevitable disappointment and suffering. The tragic dimension of life cannot be removed by planning and legislation. Instead we have to cultivate what are called 'stoic' virtues: the capacity to do without, to postpone pleasure, to make ourselves do things we do not want to do (when there is good reason to do them); to put up with minor irritations, to avoid complaint and useless criticism.

In a civilized society, these virtues are communicated and inculcated from generation to generation. There is a species of 'take control of your life' rhetoric that is superficially connected to this, but is in fact radically different. The message of 'take control' is that you will have to suffer a little now (go on a diet, be assertive, work hard), but soon, as a result, you will be successful, rich, famous and beautiful. The reality, however, is that we have to practise the stoic virtues not as a means to securing happy celebrity, but as a way of coping with tragedy. We have to be controlled, effortful, patient and uncomplaining without the expectation of any special reward.

However, there is a strange kind of reward that – though minor – is significant. If we aspire to and practise and appreciate these stoic virtues, we join company with all those who have done so before and will do so in the future. Civilization, in this respect, is a community of maturity in which across the ages individuals try to help each other cope with the demands of mortality. So, in taking this seriously, you become part of civilization in an inward and deep way.

THE COMIC SENSE

The naturalness of folly – in ourselves and others – is what fuels our sense of humour, at its best. The limited side of comedy is a form of sneering – one delights in the ridiculousness of others from a position of being above all that. Such wit is designed to support us in our difficulties – by mocking those we dislike we find it easier to cope. But there is a grander, more generous form of comedy.

One of the most civilized instances of comedy is Jerome K. Jerome's *Three Men in a Boat*. It is a book in which the joke is rarely on other people. The story follows the exploits of the writer and his two closest friends as they pass a week rowing a boat up the Thames. And this is one of the first clues as to the civilized nature of the humour: the wit emerges within – and helps to sustain – warm relationships.

There is a lovely episode near the start when the three men are attempting to pack. Each is secretly smug about his organizational skills and quietly sure the others will mess things up. In fact, collectively they make an epic failure out of what must really be a straightforward task:

'They began in a light-hearted spirit, evidently intending to show me how to do it. I made no comment; I only waited. When George is hanged Harris will be the worst packer in this world; and I looked at the piles of plates and cups, and kettles, and bottles, and jars, and pies, and stoves, and cakes, and tomatoes, etc., and felt that the thing would soon become exciting.

'It did. They started with breaking a cup. That was the first thing they did. They did that just to show you what they *could* do, and to get you interested.

'Then Harris packed the strawberry jam on top of a

tomato and squashed it, and they had to pick out the tomato with a teaspoon.

'And then it was George's turn, and he trod on the butter. I didn't say anything, but I came over and sat on the edge of the table and watched them. It irritated them more than anything I could have said. I felt that. It made them nervous and excited, and they stepped on things, and put things behind them, and then couldn't find them when they wanted them; and they packed the pies at the bottom, and put heavy things on top, and smashed the pies in.

'They upset salt over everything, and as for the butter! I never saw two men do more with one-and-twopence worth of butter in my whole life than they did. After George had got it off his slipper, they tried to put it in the kettle. It wouldn't go in, and what *was* in wouldn't come out. They did scrape it out at last, and put it down on a chair, and Harris sat on it, and it stuck to him, and they went looking for it all over the room.

' "I'll take my oath I put it down on that chair," said George, staring at the empty seat.

' "I saw you do it myself, not a minute ago," said Harris.

'Then they started round the room again looking for it; and then they met again in the centre and stared at one another.

' "Most extraordinary thing I ever heard of," said George. "So mysterious!" said Harris.

'Then George got round at the back of Harris and saw it.

' "Why, here it is all the time," he exclaimed, indignantly.

' "Where?" cried Harris, spinning round.

' "Stand still, can't you?" roared George, flying after him.

'And they got it off, and packed it in the teapot.'

*

Such an episode has little practical consequence for the reader. Despite being very fond of it, I continue to be tense and aggressive while packing. The point of the humour is retrospective. Something that was not at all funny at the time is redeemed by memory and by a way of retelling what happened so as to make it – as a story – extremely amusing.

The civilizing influence of this kind of humour – if only we can learn to do some less polished version of it ourselves – lies in its power to redeem the unpalatable, frustrating features of ordinary life. This is not revelation: it is not about learning to find incompetence entertaining. It is rather that the way events live on in our minds makes a great deal of difference to the kind of life we think we are having.

There is nothing remotely funny about being unable to get into a hotel on a rainy night, as happens to the three men in one of the most delirious sequences. But this experience – exasperating and utterly tedious as it would be in reality – becomes charming when retold once they are home. This is the secret of the book, which ends up with the three men happily having dinner back in the city, having cut short their excursion.

We're concerned, here, with the relationship between comedy and life. There is perhaps no more tender evocation of this relationship than the opening sequence of the old Mr Bean series. The bizarre, anarchic and ghastly Mr Bean is shown falling to earth, landing in a foetal position on a stony street: an image of a man utterly unarmed for the adult world. And then, rather quietly, there is music: a lovely, sober, noble choral piece. It is not soaring, or grand. It is rather like a lullaby – although less personal. But it is a hymn of love: the music of a parent's feeling towards a newborn baby: helpless, unknowing, wholly overtaken by the intense demands of its body.

Mr Bean's music lasts only for a very short time – less than thirty seconds – then we are launched into nose-picking, lavatories and world-record gaucherie.

THE EPIC ATTITUDE

The capacity for redemption through memory is one of the civilizing opportunities afforded by the fact that we do not only have experience, but we also reorganize and understand experience in a narrative form. We represent ourselves to ourselves; and this is both an astonishing burden and a great opportunity.

Civilization, in this sense, is to do with the art of memory. The art, that is, of organizing the stuff that happens to us as we grasp it after the fact. Tragedy and comedy are arts of interpreting life: they order experience – and do so in a way that makes those occurrences more bearable and more fruitful. They are ways in which memory and imagination become sources of enrichment rather than persecution.

'Epic' is the name for a crucial way in which we join up experiences over time – how we perceive the larger rhythms of life, and what kinds of patterns we think we can make out. A central instance of this epic vision is given in Virgil's *Aeneid*. We first encounter Aeneas, a Trojan prince, at a moment of crushing defeat. Troy is falling to the Greeks, the city is in flames; his friends are killed. The whole fabric of Aeneas's life is collapsing.

In the confusion he escapes. Through many adventures and in the face of innumerable difficulties, Aeneas eventually finds his way to Italy with his followers, and there, against bitter opposition, he establishes a city. It is central to this story that his descendants will be the makers of Rome. The epic narrative stretches far beyond the life of Aeneas himself, towards a heroic future – indeed to the moment when Virgil wrote his poem. It takes us from the lowest points of defeat and humiliation to the most spectacular achievements in the history of the world.

This is the epic imagination at its most hopeful: we can make sense of our difficulties because they are part of a larger vision of life within which struggle makes sense. This vision is not necessarily true: often enough we struggle in vain. A civilization is a carrier of epic meaning – both at the level of an individual life and at the level of a whole group of societies.

But civilization makes demands on epic meaning. This search for a grand, overarching story, which will make sense of life – this need for a guiding myth – is very dangerous as well as noble; dangerous because we can hitch our self-regard to stories that are false. The problem is how to civilize this impulse; how to meet the almost opposed demands of redemptive meaning (a story that is good enough, hopeful enough, to be worth believing) and plausibility (a story that is true enough, close enough to reality, to be a genuine source of strength).

The epic of today – the epic we need – is the *Bildungsroman*: the episodic study of development in individual lives.

The notion of 'Bildung' arose initially in scientific discourse. Goethe, for example (in the *Metamorphosis of Plants*, 1790), uses it to articulate the process of development whereby a seed grows into a mature plant. It was redeployed by Wilhelm von Humboldt in some essays of 1792 on the role of the state in connection with private life. 'Bildung' then became the desired process of self-development through which an individual comes to maturity and freedom. In this case, the very things that Rousseau argued were compromised by civilization (freedom and being oneself) are seen as requiring a complex society. In *Wilhelm Meister's Apprenticeship*, which was published in 1795, Goethe established the genre of the *Bildungsroman*, the novel of individual development. This work traces in detail the process of social interaction, and the sequence of errors and confusions, through which Wilhelm achieves some measure of autonomy and maturity.

With the notion of 'Bildung' and its emphasis on the private, internal development of the individual we can trace a reciprocal connection between the two principal objects of civilization: states (or societies) and individuals. It is the responsibility of the state to provide for (or at least not interfere with) the development of the individual, and the good state or society needs to be governed by individuals who have themselves developed in this way. This, at least, was von Humboldt's thesis.

18

Little Things

The ancient Greek moralist Theophrastus coined a useful term: 'microphilotimos' – which means 'attaching importance to unimportant things'. This illuminates the third of the key themes of civilization, as sketched in the imaginary chat-show discussion in Chapter 1.

Theophrastus would have been interested in a modern attempt to use his ideas as a help in everyday life. Richard Carlson's *Don't Sweat the Small Stuff* reminds us that many of the things that worry and upset us are not terribly important. Being late for a dental appointment is a favourite example. And, if we could see how unimportant these things truly are, we would enjoy a better life. But an insight into what constitutes the small stuff is hard to come by. One recommendation is to ask yourself: 'Will this matter in a hundred years' time?' The conclusion, when it comes to missing a dental appointment, is pretty obvious. But this question is not a helpful one: by this standard nothing matters. Apart from maximizing one's offspring.

Or, if one is like Richard Wagner, the message is too exciting. The great German composer was obsessed by luxury, which he considered necessary if he were to coax himself into the right frame of mind for writing music. But for much of his life he had a tiny income and he borrowed from all his friends and acquaintances, with little thought about how he would repay the money. After all, he would have reasoned, what does it matter if I borrow heavily from this person and do not pay them back? They are ruined, so what? Who will care in a hundred years' time?

The issue cannot be: How can we ignore the small stuff? – since much of life actually requires us to attend to it. It is better to ask: How can the little things in life gain in stature? How do they become meaningful? The ambition to civilize life is – here – the hope that we can find convincing (not just pretend) ways in which the ordinary activities of daily life can be given importance.

This is what lies behind our third speaker's anecdote from Tolstoy. The character Oblonsky pays a lot of attention to little things: How is the fish cooked? What temperature is the champagne? His view is that 'the whole aim of civilization is to make everything a source of enjoyment'. And he then puts many philosophers to shame by his easy passage from theory to practice, turning to the waiter and asking for: three dozen oysters, clear soup, turbot, roast beef, capons and (to our ears a naive touch) fruit salad, champagne and two bottles of Chablis.

In a fashion, Oblonsky is right. How we deal with little things and how we enjoy ourselves are crucial to civilization. But there are so many ways these can go wrong, so we reach only another question: What is the civilized way to deal with little things?

A civilizing process is one in which some existing need or impulse develops well so that it serves our higher, nobler longings. Conversation is the civilization of speech; love is the civilization of sex; friendship is the civilization of loyalty. One extremely powerful existing impulse, or need, is towards material prosperity. But if we see this as the equivalent of speech or sex, what would the drive to material prosperity look like if it were civilized? The civilization of that drive would not diminish it, but would make it stronger, more important, more valuable to us; but what sort of development, what sort of process of transformation, would bring this about, and where would it lead us?

The root notion of a civilizing process is this: some part of life is developed and improved. What this means is that this improved part of life becomes a vehicle for other values, as well as for achieving its own particular purpose. It is integrated, as it were, with the further concerns of meaning, with other values and purposes that we want to pursue in life. An activity becomes an art.

We get a good view of the civilizing process in the Japanese tea ceremony. Although, of course, it is culturally specific, the historical development of the ceremony reveals something universal. Tea was first considered as a medicine; then it became more widespread as a pleasing hot drink. By the fifteenth century, a ceremony had developed around the drinking of tea. While retaining its material virtues as a soothing and refreshing liquid, tea also came to have a spiritual meaning. A conception of life found its focus here: the apparently minor acts of preparing and drinking gradually became richer in significance, expressing a view of the human condition.

One thing that happened was that perception became more acute: more care and attention were devoted to the particular utensils, to the length of time one might spend over a cup of tea, to the kinds of conversation that you might have. In some form or another of course you have to use something to drink out of, you have to take some amount of time to drink it, and have to have some ideas running through your head. The evolution of the tea ceremony took up these necessary factors – these inescapable elements of ordinary activity – and invited those who participated in it to be ambitious about them.

Tea, in Japan, was not an especially luxurious drink; and this theme was developed. The tea ceremony understood and took seriously the pleasures of being economical. And in line with this, there is an emphasis upon simplicity. The materials should be plain and ordinary.

Drinking a cup of tea is, essentially, a transient activity: the steam curls upwards and disappears; the drink cools; time passes. And before very long you will be thirsty again. The ritual of the ceremony guides the participant to be conscious of time, to pay attention to the pace and rhythm of action.

And the drinking of tea is itself a respite – a self-conscious moment of idleness – away from the demands and constraints of duty and business. It should be a quietly convivial occasion; and part of its meaning is that life cannot always be like this.

Of course, the pleasures of economy – of the careful use of resources – the consideration of the passing of time, can be brought to our attention in other ways. It is not that we need a tea ceremony to pay attention to these things. The lesson of the tea ceremony is not that we should copy it exactly. The lesson is that we can take fairly minor ordinary activities and raise them to a higher meaning. And in doing so we are not merely projecting or pretending. When the civilizing process goes well, the deeper significance of daily life – as the arena in which the meaning of life is played out – becomes apparent and gets the recognition it deserves. Our ordinary activities become the arts of everyday life.

Curiously, you cannot really enter into these arts just by

knowing about them from the outside. You could understand, as an observer, rather a lot about the 'meaning' of
each part of the ceremony – now they are waiting for the
water to boil: this is a symbol of the need for patience. But
that is not at all the same as participating in the ceremony.
Participation requires an inward alignment – a conviction
that this matters to you. The experience that it is right: the
feeling that it has to be done this way. Not that other
people think it right.

In the development of an art form, more and more elements
that are – almost of necessity – used in the creation of
an object become the foci of self-conscious ambitions. A
picture, for example, must of necessity have a boundary:
the canvas must stop somewhere. But that brute fact can –
at some stage – be taken up and used for further purposes:
the position of figures relative to the edge becomes a theme.
Or – to take a further example – the different parts must
have some colours: this can be developed self-consciously;
the harmony or dissonance of the colours is no longer a
matter of chance: it becomes a resource for increasing the
significance and the visual merits of the work. Any element
can be developed; and the greater the number of elements
thematized in this way, the richer the art form becomes.
(One can, in fact, see this process being enacted in the
artistic education of children.) But that – in turn – raises
the difficulty of how the thematized elements are to be
controlled and organized; the accumulation of resources of
meaning, on its own, does not in itself lead to the creation
of anything fine: it might just lead to chaos. So, overarching
goals and ambitions, which tie the object to the wider
demands and concerns of life, have to develop.

*

It is this process that explains and justifies the development of manners. People become more self-conscious about the physical actions that they perform: How are you moving your arm? Which actions are you performing simultaneously? What sounds are you making? What implements are you using? These can then be related to wider goals: hygiene and digestion, privacy, not being disturbed, not disturbing, conviviality, aesthetic goals such as elegance and style, concerns with efficiency. These do not necessarily fit together easily, but a style of manners evolves to hold them together.

What this means is that the development of manners need not just be a set of arbitrary changes: at best it is to do with raising up the ambition that attaches to a normal process, such as eating. And that process goes wrong if the ambition simply burdens it with a set of expectations and rituals that do not really serve higher needs. Hence certain modes of 'good manners' can be rightly criticized and mocked, without this leaving the idea of good manners as such in the wilderness.

In Evelyn Waugh's *Brideshead Revisited* there is a memorable soliloquy in which the dying earl describes the collective achievements of his ancestors. They ploughed the land, they drained the marshes, planted corn and fattened their cattle. One man built the mansion house; his son spread the colonnades. His son, in turn, added the dome, and another descendant dammed the river to make a wonderful lake. It is a deeply appealing image of accumulation, generations collaborate in an enterprise far greater and finer than any they could have carried out individually.

There is a pathos to this particular man's remarks because he is not party to this process of addition; he has squandered a large part of his inheritance; he has failed to renew its vigour – he is no longer active in the world (he merely sits on it). Most bitterly, he has neglected its passage into the future – his heirs are ill-equipped to bear such a fortune.

We should not be misled by the specifically aristocratic and wealthy dress of this story. Like a magnifying glass, it allows us to see blown up to great size processes that generally occur in less obvious, less noticeable, forms.

In essence this tale points to a process of good accumulation. A process that is central to the civilized vision of a good individual life and a good society. Accumulation is one hopeful story of existence – not the only story. Its outer, material narrative is a proxy – sometimes a pale substitute – for an inward process, in which each object, each addition, really does add to and enrich what was already there.

What we hold on to – what grows in us – is a kind of sediment, deposited by the objects we love. Each thing adds not only to our physical environment, but also to the gradual creation of who we are. The relations of the parts become richer and deeper – more true to who we are in our better moments. It builds up, gradually, as a holding environment, as what it holds gradually builds. This conversation and building up is what we call style; it is the outward aspect of what should be in concert with an inward process – a process which it leads, guides, supports and expresses. On the grandest level, a civilization is the public equivalent of this.

Accumulation is a possessive metaphor. It suggests how things come to belong to us: how they add up. But we know that adding up – in life – is not a matter of just heaping one thing on top of another. It is not to do with clutter or heaps: our words for disordered multiplicity.

Good accumulation is personal architecture: the art of making things work together; the art of composition. This is something we face inescapably if only because life is quite long and complicated. We want the mass of experience to add together. So, a society is civilized to the degree that it helps us in this fundamental task.

It is said of Poussin – one of the most thoughtful of painters – that he owned only nineteen books. Of course this was in the early seventeenth century – an era when personal libraries were much smaller than today and books were luxury items. But still it is a beguiling idea: to have only a few books, but each one to be fine and serious, and to read them again and again – to get to know intimately and deeply what they are about. Rereading allows for the thoughts in them and one's own thoughts to grow together: for the secrets of the works to be carefully and slowly appraised, for their content to be thought over and thought through.

This image is an antidote to the feeling of dissipation – of intellectual dissipation – which comes from trying to assimilate too much too quickly.

It is an imaginative failing if we see refinement only as fussiness, preciousness and too easily offended delicacy. Refinement comes in as part of the civilizing process. It is one of the ideas – one of the routes – for converting a mass of stuff into the house of life. That is because refinement is what we call sharpening our sense of relevance: sharpening our sense of what we need and why, and shaping our sense of what is on offer. What does the experience or object really mean? What does it really offer for life? It is like knowing better what resources we need. The shadow side of refinement apes this sharpness but does not catch the point. Shadow refinement has only a low, social ambition – to appear sophisticated. The real point of sophistication is to do things that require sophistication but which serve good purpose.

In this sense a person is civilized when they have developed a capacity for good refinement. And a society is civilized to the degree that it helps people develop this capacity. That is, to the degree that it helps us live by a distinction between faux and real sophistications and faux and real refinement.

The degree of civilization that a particular society has can be gauged by asking a key question: To what extent does that society support, foster and spread good accumulation and this kind of refinement?

In 1728 the young French painter Chardin was elected to the Academy in Paris. At that time, painters were admitted to particular grades within the Academy, and these grades had a strict hierarchy. At the top were the artists who produced 'history paintings'; below them were the portrait painters; then the landscape painters; the lowest rung was occupied by those who painted still-life and animal pictures – and it was to this echelon that Chardin was admitted.

This system derived from what was known as the 'hierarchy of the genres'. Although hardly fashionable today, the hierarchy was based on some quite reasonable principles. The point was that some painters deal with more important subject matter than others. A picture of an obviously important event, and couched in the most serious of moral terms, must surely be a more valuable thing – a greater human achievement – than the creation of a likeness of a bowl of cherries or a dead rabbit.

However, within his lifetime Chardin became one of the most revered and highly respected of artists. How did this happen? Not by Chardin changing his subject matter – rather, by a growing recognition that the portrayal of apparently humble subject matter could be a vehicle for meditation upon themes of the largest significance. To put it crudely: Chardin's pictures of cherries and the like are not 'about' fruit – they are ways of trying to grasp the nature of existence. These are pictures that evoke a sense of repose, of contented solitude, of contemplative appreciation of moments of time.

Consider, for example, Chardin's picture of a lady drinking tea. It shows us a tranquil, meditative moment in which a woman pauses as she raises a spoon to stir her tea. The steam rises from the cup. It is a magically attractive picture: What is it trying to tell us? What is it hinting at?

At one level, all she is doing is hydrating her body. What we see is the way in which a necessary activity has been elaborated and made into an art. She is civilized because of how she is doing a very ordinary thing. And, strikingly, she is civilized not because of any special luxury or material grandeur – in fact the cup is fairly unremarkable, the table is nothing special. She is civilized because she is attentive, appreciative; she has found a way of making this activity beautiful. She is making the most of this bit of life. One aim of civilization is to spread this style of behaviour across more and more of the details of life.

In these cases we see what could be merely utilitarian activities (getting things to eat; getting across water) develop in complex and subtle ways – not so much that they become harder to do (they actually become easier, with practice). Rather, doing them well becomes an arena in which being a good person is enacted.

We have seen the notion of sublimation (the raising of the lower to the higher) in connection with impressive objects. But here we see the same essential project undertaken with respect to apparently minor or trivial things.

Care, authority, direction and focus of attention, the accumulation of experience, the winnowing of the essential from the irrelevant: these show that it is not so much what type of action as the way that it is developed that is crucial. These are examples of 'quality of relationship' – and the things undertaken participate in a higher realm of meaning and value. They become important to us in a new way.

The central ambition of the civilizing process is to develop – and improve – the quality of our relationships. We have relationships to ideas, places, people, objects, difficulties and opportunities, memories, ambitions. Indeed, the character of a life is largely determined by how these relationships go. The most forlorn – but frequently experienced – is when we relate in an impoverished or unhelpful way to something that, in principle, has a lot to offer. The history of a nation, for example, is something each person relates to in their own way. In some cases, however, that relationship might be very intense, but fundamentally of a low quality. Words like 'obsession', 'fantasy', 'wilful blindness' are terms that capture poor relationships. Ideas of great potential, with all the depth and difficulty of another person, can be flattened and reduced in our minds by how we see them. Just as the most interesting and thoughtful person will be nothing to us – will not become a friend or an inspiration or a real colleague – unless we can find the resources in ourselves that help that relationship to flower.

The notion of quality of relationship has something to say about us when we are the ones who are reaching out and relating: What resources of imagination, understanding, invention and perception do we bring to the relationship? Have we got what it takes to make the relationship flower? But quality of relationship also depends crucially on the qualities of the thing we are reaching out to and engaging with. As with some human relationships, it does not matter how much we bring: there is nowhere for it to go: the person is just too difficult, too limited, too demanding, too stunted for a good relationship to evolve. (Or it may be that the fault lies in us.)

So, as we grow in our capacity to relate – in our capacity to love – we need to find people and objects with which we can sustain and develop more rewarding, richer and more valuable relationships. I think we understand this quite well in some areas of life: a job, for instance, might become too limited, too simple, to be rewarding to us; as we develop we have to find more suitable opportunities. But the same holds true of our relationships to ideas and to works of art.

19

Raising Up

Perhaps the most illuminating discussion of what we might call a civilizing process occurred in the Middle Ages. In the face of the imperfections of the world, the serious and refined person is tempted to withdraw. What is noble and pure and truly important cannot survive in the rough world or in the market place. It has to have a sanctuary; and those who wish to enter have to undertake an arduous process of purification. This approach was mapped out in the twelfth century by Bernard of Clairvaux. 'No secular person is allowed direct access to the House of God.' The merely curious are barred from seeing the sacred objects; the monastery maintains a 'silence and perpetual remoteness from all secular turmoil and compels the mind to meditate on celestial things'. In certain moods this sounds delightful.

According to Bernard there is nothing one can do to make the good popular. It is not that he actively wants to exclude people – he is not glad that only a few can appreciate what is excellent. But he holds that what is serious and fine requires devotion and care on the part of anyone who wishes to grasp it. Thus, in terms of the modern world, he is a representative figure for a certain kind of pessimism. Sensitive and serious people have to retreat. In the Middle Ages, refuge was in the austere cloister; today it might be a university department; or it might just be a lower standard of living: the consequence of a refusal to compete in the uncouth world.

At the time not everyone agreed with Bernard. His most interesting opponent was a rival clerical leader, the Abbot Suger. I worried for a long time about the pronunciation of his name; I emailed a few specialists and this was the most helpful reply: 'I believe one pronounces the word SUE-jay with tongue further back to the middle of the mouth on the j to produce a more French-sounding z rather than j as jam.'

Suger was born in 1081: his parents were poor but he was adopted into the abbey community of St-Denis from an early age and educated at its famous school, where he formed a close friendship with his future sovereign, Louis VI, 'the Fat'. The abbey had strong connections to the crown: it was the traditional burial place of the French kings. It held extensive lands, but these were poorly managed. The buildings had been neglected; the church treasures had been pledged as surety for loans.

Suger began his career as an economic administrator; in his late twenties he was appointed to oversee a once valuable estate that had been laid waste by lawless local barons; the peasants had fled, merchants avoided the area. A slight, frail man, Suger was amazingly energetic and resourceful. He fortified the estate buildings, drafted an army of parishioners, besieged the oppressors' castle – which he eventually destroyed – constructed new buildings, established new farms, vineyards and plantations and regulated local taxation. His zeal and competence led him to be appointed as abbot of St-Denis and later as regent of France while the king was absent on Crusade.

But Suger was much more than just a high-ranking, gifted civil servant. He pursued economic and administrative goals because he wished the Church to flourish – for which material wealth was necessary but not sufficient. He devoted the wealth of his abbey to the creation of a new, and very splendid, abbey church. In pursuit of intense sensory impact he developed some of the leading motifs of Gothic architecture: the soaring interior; the expanses of stained glass; the rose window above the main doors.

The idea behind all this magnificence was that people could be helped by all sorts of inducements, sweeteners and encouragements to rise from low-grade enthusiasms to a more sophisticated understanding and profound appreciation. Suger wanted to make his abbey church as noble and grand as possible – and to bring in as many people as possible to see it, and in this he was extremely successful. Under his guidance, St-Denis gained great spiritual authority. His achievement illuminates a distinction that is absolutely crucial for civilization: that between popularization and populism. We should not be distracted by the fact that Suger is concerned specifically with religious worship: the point is to do with enthusing and inducting a wider audience into an appreciative relation to something that he and all intelligent people of the era regarded as deeply important.

Populism frankly asserts that whatever people happen to like is just fine. Suger does not take his lead from others; he is not making up his view of life to fit what people happen to want. He is engaged in a much more interesting and relevant project. He has a firm and immensely serious conception of what is really important. He then asks – in a sympathetic rather than irritated voice – how this noble vision can be presented to people who are not yet ready for the full, pure blast. How can more people be brought towards it? He thinks that charm is the key.

In his thinking about reaching a broad audience, Suger had to hand two very helpful ideas. The beauty and charm of material things are particularly accessible to a wide audience – their appeal is obvious and natural; but, at the same time, they urge us on from material to immaterial things.

One: 'There is a formidable distance between the highest, purely intelligible sphere of existence to the lowest, almost purely material one; but there is no insurmountable chasm between the two. There is hierarchy, not dichotomy. For even the lowliest things partake somehow of the essence of God – that is (humanly speaking), of the qualities of truth, goodness and beauty.'

Two: 'Therefore the process by which the emanations of the Light Divine flow down until they are nearly drowned in matter and broken up into what looks like a meaningless welter of coarse material bodies can always be reversed into a rise from pollution and multiplicity to purity and oneness.'

Together, these beliefs framed what Suger was doing. They allowed him to believe that appreciation can rise from quite basic and sensual origins to a noble ethical ideal. And his task, as he saw it, was to help people accomplish this ascent in their own lives. The lesser things do not fall away as we rise; their worth is raised too, for we find more and more in them; they become eloquent not only of material beauty but also of spiritual beauty.

He also held that all members of his congregation – whether learned or ignorant, noble or lowly, morally upright or wicked – had an immortal soul; that the destiny of this soul was far more important than anything else; and that salvation was not won by the intellect, but by love. Suger was a great respecter of learning – and his own writings reveal him to be highly educated. Learning is a help, but not in itself the aim. What Suger is pointing to is really a vision of growth; and he is trusting in that he takes it for granted that this kind of development is almost always possible. He was heir to a religious tradition that wholly supported this idea. The idea of the soul – which Christianity developed in the light of Plato – envisages everyone as having a profound and serious destiny. However rough and brutish the exterior and the actions may be, there must always remain lodged somewhere, buried no matter how deeply, a set of inescapable needs: this person must still long for love, for knowledge, for completion and for happiness.

Suger – like all heroes of civilization – does not belong only to his own time. The issue that concerned him is of central importance for civilization today: How can a wide audience be gained for ideals that – in their pure form – are daunting? How can quality and quantity be reconciled?

Suger's critics saw him as vain and worldly. And in fact he was these things: he derived great personal satisfaction from the material success of his administration; he did devote a great deal of his attention to activities that might more readily be associated with a merchant or a prince than with a churchman. But the criticism rests upon the false assumption that his personal aggrandisement and his enthusiasm for money and power are at odds with his devotion to noble ideals. Was his idealism merely a polite, respectable screen for his venial preoccupations?

In fact, Suger shows us something which is of the greatest modern importance. His primary concern is to raise people from mass to elite culture. And his way of doing this is not by being snobbish or hard on ordinary enjoyments. He takes the view that mass culture is just an undeveloped, beginning way of addressing exactly the same things that high culture serves more directly and with greater insight. (*The Secret* is philosophy for the uneducated; *Trash Talk* – an internet gossip site – is Tolstoy for beginners.) We desperately need to bring to inner development the sort of clarity and respectability that goes with making your way in the material world.

20

Barbarism . . .

In a curious maxim La Rochefoucauld claims that 'it is harder to bear great fortune than great misfortune'. It is an annoying remark because the important point – that it is hard to bear great fortune – is embedded in a spurious contrast. It would be enough to point out that it is quite hard to bear good fortune; whether it is harder than bearing misfortune is not a question we have an urgent need to settle.

Behind this remark lies a general point. The greater the resources or powers we possess, the greater our opportunity to inflict good or evil upon others or ourselves. But La Rochefoucauld is not merely pointing out that good fortune (the possession of powers and resources) brings responsibilities: what he is getting at is that it is especially hard to exercise responsibility well – hence it is 'hard to bear'.

This is a submerged issue in modern times. Particularly, we lay such stress on acquiring power and resources, fame and money, that we do not much notice that the ways in which people get these things may have little connection to the task of using them well. Money is gained by luck through inheritance, by competitive drive in the market place, by efficiency in servicing the wants of others, by speculation and gambling. But none of these has any bearing upon the good use of resources once you have them.

Echoing this maxim: Civilization depends upon undertaking the hard task of using good fortune well. Civilization depends upon the possession of a wide range of material resources – the technical capacities, the legislation, the economic opportunities that so impressed the thinkers of the Enlightenment – but it does not depend only upon those resources. It is also a question of the ideals and ambitions that govern and guide the use of the capacities we have.

We can gain a clearer sense of what is at stake – regarding the guiding ideals and ambitions – by considering the meaning of 'barbarism' and 'decadence'.

The word 'barbarism' has an unpromising, faintly idiotic, origin. It was coined in ancient Greece as a way of mocking those who did not belong to Hellenic culture and who did not speak one of the Greek dialects. The speech of the incomprehensible foreigner was regarded as little better than the bleating of a sheep: baa-baa-barbarian.

However, this smug provincial attitude was not as secure as it might seem. The 'barbarians' about whom the Greeks were most concerned were the Persians. The Persians were highly sophisticated, they had the same level of technology as the Greeks, they could put large armies in the field and fleets on the seas; their kings had vast economic resources, greater than those of any of the Greek states. So despite its original mocking overtone, 'barbarian' was not a term that applied to people in a weak position. A barbarian could be a powerful, ferocious, and very possibly victorious, enemy.

Building on this, the term 'barbarism' developed a further, very useful, meaning in the second half of the nineteenth century. Now, it began to be clear, the barbarians were not so much people on the outside, as a powerful and important group within modern developed societies.

This was how Matthew Arnold employed the term: 'When I go through the country and see this and that beautiful and imposing seat of the aristocratic class crowning the landscape, "There," I say to myself, "is a great fortified post of the Barbarians."'

The barbarians were certainly not people who lacked resources or power; they were healthy, vigorous, chivalrous; they were marked by 'courage, high spirits and self-confidence'; they prized health and good looks. What, one might wonder, can Arnold find to fault them on? In what sense are they barbarians?

Well, this: their outward accomplishments and possessions – their great material prosperity – are not well directed. They do not serve any higher purpose than their own maintenance. In other words, barbarians have a very high degree of material prosperity but no corresponding spiritual prosperity.

This is an important insight, for it distances us from the worry that civilization is just another name for the way of life of those who happen to be at the top of any social pile. What is so liberating here is that we are being asked to see a group of people, who might otherwise be thought to be the chief representatives of civilization, as in fact lacking a crucial element of true civilization. They have the externals, but not the inner spirit. In other words, the problem of barbarism is a lack of proportion between the resources to hand and the moral or imaginative capacity to use those resources constructively and well. The barbarian hordes, who so terrorized the later years of the Roman Empire, possessed great resources: they had large armies, immense energy and determination; they acquired immense quantities of plunder. They constructed nothing.

. . . and Decadence

Decadence occurs in its purest form when a society is no longer capable of maintaining itself. In a memorable poem W. H. Auden describes the nightmarish situation in which decadence meets with barbarism.

> Read on, ambassador, engrossed
> In your favourite Stendhal;
> The Outer Provinces are lost,
> Unshaven horsemen swill
> The great wines of the Chateaux
> Where you danced long ago.

The ambassador is the representative of a society – or, at least, of the leading group in a society – that has been unable to hold on to the resources it once commanded and put to good use. He can still read Stendhal; and the reference is an apt one. For Stendhal, while among the most charming and intimate of authors, is a great artist of his own weakness. His sensitivity was so acute that he was often incapable of action: his romantic affairs were paralysed from the beginning, but he never had the strength to break them off; he moped for years – although he writes about it with unequalled sweetness and candour.

While the horsemen can capture the fine houses, and

seize the wines, they have no appreciation of what has fallen into their hands. However much they enjoy drinking, they will not tend the vines. They consume but they cannot create. The historical frame of the verse is complex. 'The Outer Provinces' refers, perhaps, to the decline of the Roman Empire; while the 'Chateaux' and 'Stendhal' make more sense in terms of the Franco-Prussian War of 1870 – when the victorious Prussian officers, billeted in the grand houses around Paris, delighted in destroying as much as they could. German propaganda paintings of the time present this violence as the assertion of straightforward manly energy, rightfully sweeping away the fussy weakness of French sophistication: the muddy boots trampling the fine carpets, the massive frames of the cavalry corps putting to shame the mincingly delicate furniture.

The ambassador is decadent, and belongs to a decadent society, because his refinement is no help in the present emergency. This is why Auden needs the Roman Empire association: it is not a sign of decadence to be suddenly overpowered by an unexpected attack, as the French were in 1870. The poem needs to carry an implication of negligence. Hence 'Read on': he has been reading Stendhal – and only doing that, apart from the occasional bout of ballroom dancing – all his adult life.

The distorted historical references invite us to regard the poem as describing a problem that can arise at any point, including now. And barbarism and decadence need not be assigned to different societies but can coexist and feed each other in a single society. The real task for the ambassador, and the sophisticated culture that he represents, is to educate the barbaric forces at work in his own society. If the cultivated elite simply 'read on . . . engrossed', then how can the energetic drives of the society be anything other than barbaric?

Modern decadence lies in a sense of weakness – of being unable to connect high culture to the demands of daily life and with any powerful or pragmatic sense of continuity and renewal.

The roots of barbarism lie in a dangerously narrow sense of meaning. The wine has nothing to say to the barbarian except: I can make you intoxicated; the painting has nothing to say except: I cost a lot of money, or I express your pride in ancestry; the big house says: I have a lot of money. The points of connection are extremely simple and limited. And this can occur even though the objects in question have – in principle – vastly more to offer. Barbarism kills things in imagination even before it puts them to the flame; and puts them to the flame because it cannot think of anything more interesting to do with them.

Barbarism is not a lack of power – it is unbridled, unprincipled power; power in the absence of reason, virtue and taste.

For a long time, the opposite of civilization was thought to be savage life; as if these were the only options. And that always looked rather unbalanced; for whatever the imagined or real attractions of pre-industrial societies, that form of life was always going to be immensely vulnerable: civilization, whatever its actual merits, would always have the money, resources, firepower, technology and organization to take over any society that happened to be primitive in those areas – irrespective of the other virtues and attractions that society might possess.

So, in this way of thinking, civilization can come across

as the bully; it is the strong-armed bit of the world. But the real opposition is actually between civilization and barbarism. Civilization can be defeated by barbarism. This is an important shift in perspective because it cleans away the temptation to confuse civilization with the powers that be – the name that powerful societies happen to give themselves.

The key task for civilization is the conversion of barbarism and decadence. With respect to barbarism, the task is really to do with enriching self-awareness. The limited outlook of the barbarian derives from having few ideas about what might matter personally. Lack of sensitivity to others and to the world is grounded in a lack of sensitivity to oneself. And typically the barbarian feels that there is no space for sensitivity: it will lead to defeat or humiliation. The toughness, the bravado, of barbarism is a thesis about the world: this is what it takes to succeed or to survive.

With respect to decadence, the task is to do with generating hope. Decadence is defeatism before the consequences of defeat have been felt: it is sensitivity that recoils from supporting itself in the mixed condition of the world. What both need, from civilization, is friendship.

Barbarism is strength without sensitivity; decadence is sensitivity without strength. And the lack, in each case, damages the virtue. In the absence of sensitivity, strength is blind – it blunders about, destructive and menacing. In the absence of strength, sensitivity is vulnerable, morose, paralysed.

The basic error in response to decadence is to criticize it as a form of laziness; in reality it is disguised despair, which cannot be fixed by stern words. The basic error in response to barbarism is contempt; but crudity cannot cure itself, and contempt does not offer the barbarian any help. In each case, the response is a failure of friendship.

What are the causes of barbarism? One: the fear that any check upon one's appetites will be unendurable. Hence: I must drink as much as possible, have as much sex as possible and scream my desires at the world. Two: radical impatience. Hence: if I try to explain I'll get nowhere, if I negotiate I'll be outwitted, if I hesitate I'll be attacked. Three: intense fear of humiliation. By the standards of civilized people I am disgusting; therefore I shall destroy civilization. Four: conformism. My tribe acts like this, so I will act like this. Five: fear of boredom. I cannot think of anything good to do, but I have to do something. Six: the need for obvious markers. How do I know I am a good person? I have got 'in your face' signs of my worth – I have to show off because if I do not you will not notice me.

What are the causes of decadence? Fear: if I compete, I will be defeated. Two: lack of confidence. What I care about is not truly valuable, therefore its worth cannot be grasped by others; there is no such thing as education, just imposition – and that is not a strategy for one as weak as me. Three: romantic pessimism. I know I am a good person because I am defeated by the world. Four: communicative anxiety. I cannot tell you what is important to me because it is too subtle and elusive for you to understand, so you will just have to kick me. How do I know I am intelligent? No one understands me.

Friendship – here – relies on empathy. Empathy means holding on to the barbaric and decadent aspects of oneself. It is with inside knowledge that one addresses the barbarian or the decadent. It is the capacity to hold on to the sense that these can seem like solutions to the question: What should I do? Smash things up or do nothing? It is boring to talk to someone who cannot empathize. The civilized person is not someone who is utterly different from the barbarian or the decadent. On the contrary, a civilized person has barbarian and decadent aspects, but these have been overcome, educated and reassured.

PART FOUR

Civilization as Spiritual Prosperity

22

Life-Giving Ideas

Like many people my thoughts about civilization and civilized life have been influenced by Kenneth Clark's magnificent television series *Civilization*, first broadcast by the BBC in 1969. (I did not see it at the time – I was three and my parents did not think to sit me down in front of it. But I have made up for that since by watching it often on DVD.) The programmes show the pageant of great works of art, fine buildings, music and poetry, and the deep thoughts and feelings that went into them, that have been created in the West since the fall of the Roman Empire to the twentieth century.

The series takes up the notion of civilization as intimately connected to art: the fourth strand in our imagined late-night discussion about the idea of civilization.

These programmes could give the impression that being civilized requires having a lot of art and high-cultural information to hand: living in splendid quarters, swanning about Rome or Paris; knowing about Descartes and German rococo church architecture. This impression was totally contrary to Clark's real ambition. He wanted to show – rightly – that being civilized is to do with internalizing and using 'life-giving ideas'. Those ideas have often found their most emphatic expression in great works of art. But the ideas do not belong just to the art. Life-giving ideas belong in our lives, not on the walls of galleries. Civilization is not – must not be – the morgue of lifeless treasures, telling us something diverting about how things once were in distant times.

In the ninth episode – entitled 'The Pursuit of Happiness' – Clark takes us to eighteenth-century Germany to look at a church known as the Vierzehnheiligen: the fourteen saints. The outside is pleasant but unremarkable. The interior, however, is spectacular. It is composed of a series of interlocking ovals, with bounding arches at the intersections; the white walls are laced with gold and lift gently to sumptuous painted domes. The whole place is airy and yet magnificent; it is devoted to the most serious possible purpose (human salvation) and yet it is delightful. It gives visible expression to one of the central 'life-giving ideas' of civilization. The idea is, as Clark beautifully puts it, that one might be 'persuaded not by fear but by joy'.

The building plays out this idea in a very specific way. It seeks to persuade us by the elegance and exuberance of interior architecture: by the happiness of space and light. And it tries to convince us about something very particular: the doctrine of Catholicism. But the life-giving idea is tethered to neither the specific means nor the particular doctrine.

The intimate meaning of the idea – the resonance in life of being 'persuaded not by fear but by joy' – might become vivid when reading an angry, bitter piece of correspondence on the letters page of a newspaper. Here is someone who is trying to persuade via fear. One can easily imagine how this has come about; it is normal, when deeply upset, to try to force one's views on others in a hectoring manner. With that experience clearly in mind, one can feel how civilized, how helpful, the idea of persuading by joy really is.

Or in the aftermath of a domestic row, one might recognize that for years one has been trying to bludgeon one's partner into a change of attitude or behaviour by fear: by showing how irrational, wicked, small-minded or stupid they are. The idea of persuading by joy becomes a great principle of hope; a reorientation of effort and a prospect that we might still be able to be happy together.

The idea is bigger than the building. And that is one of the reasons why you do not need to be an eighteenth-century German Catholic to fall in love with it or for it to have something powerful and intimate to offer you. The building does not just address our historical curiosity, it offers us something that matters when we are thinking of writing a furious letter to the press or getting caught up in a domestic brawl. So, to appreciate the building, we need to bring those aggressive, fearful parts of ourselves into contact with it.

Another of Clark's 'life-giving ideas' is developed in his discussion of Rembrandt (which comes in episode eight, 'The Light of Experience'). Rembrandt, he argues, is a visual poet of 'truth and the appeal to experience'. So, when we contemplate one of Rembrandt's late self-portraits we are presented not just with a fairly accurate record of what that particular man happened to look like in late middle age; we are also faced with an attitude of self-awareness and reflection, with a search for self-knowledge, which is much bigger than this particular work. It matters in the dead of night when we wake and think of the utter strangeness of being alive: Who am I? What is my life about? What have I done with my existence?

Civilization is importantly connected to art. That is

because great works of art encapsulate ideas and experiences that are of wide significance. Clark's analysis of life-giving ideas supports this view. And it shows that civilization does not depend merely upon the existence of the works – but on how we approach them, engage with them and use them.

In *Another Part of the Wood* (1974), the second and final volume of his memoirs, Kenneth Clark describes a personal moment of crisis. *Civilization* had just been screened in America and Clark was in Washington to talk about the series. He was greeted as a hero: five thousand people turned up to a lecture; before he even spoke, they cheered him again and again. When the talk was over Clark rushed to the lavatory, locked himself in a cubicle and howled with anguish. The rapturous reception had left him in a state of intense distress. But why? What was upsetting him so much?

The explanation is given in a quiet sentence that comes much earlier in the book. He feared that his hugely successful popularization was a betrayal: an enormous, elemental lie. It was – he thought – impossible that these cheering people could genuinely love the works he had introduced them to; he feared that what they were so delighted by was that he had destroyed the high, secret wonder of the works and hawked the remnants to the multitude – who were now wildly pleased. And, even worse, they were cheering him, when he was only the nightwatchman, as it were, in the temple of great art; they were not supposed to be enthusiastic about him, but enthusiastic about the things he loved; and wild cheering could hardly be an appropriate response to that.

Clark was fond of quoting one of the bleakest – most

magnificently impressive – passages of Macbeth's self-examination and reflection on the human condition:

> Out, out, brief candle;
> Life's but a walking shadow; a poor player
> That struts and frets his hour upon the stage
> And then is heard no more: it is a tale
> Told by an idiot; full of sound and fury,
> Signifying nothing.

What would it mean to take this seriously? Not necessarily to agree with it, but to enter into it; to see it as expressing a very awkward aspect of being human: our intense desire that life should be meaningful can give way to an appalling sense that life is totally meaningless. The lines are shocking in their bluntness; glorious in their honesty, verve of expression and sense of touching something elemental. It is a solemn call to self-examination, a cry from one desperate man to which we might respond with recognition. But however impressed one might be, cheering is not exactly a plausible response.

Nor would cheering be an appropriate way of meeting the achievements of many of Clark's other heroes. What would cheering crowds mean to the inward solitude and melancholy of Wordsworth in his little isolated cottage? What Clark finds in Wordsworth is this: 'simple people and animals often show more courage and loyalty and unselfishness than sophisticated people, and also a greater sense of the wholeness of life'. This is a thought which, if taken seriously, could change a life. It is a call to a way of living. One might – as Clark himself did – resist it and yet feel, every day, its drag upon one's conscience. It is a deeply sobering and solemn claim.

And what would cheering mean in the face of the

astonishing dignity and refinement of Raphael's *The School of Athens*? In this fresco we are shown the finest creative minds in contemplative and conversational groups. Raphael himself is modest and minor. This is a work not only of homage, but also of assertion: it asserts a hierarchy of the mind in which a figure like Raphael – so famous today – sees himself as occupying only a little space. So where is the viewer? It is meant to be a humbling, as well as inspiring, work. To take it seriously is to recognize one's own littleness, perhaps to be inspired to great devotion. But how do the people cheering Clark stand in relation to this noble vision? Are they moved by the truth of Raphael or are they – inadvertently and with the kindest of intentions – its enemies?

23

Down in the City

I arrived in Florence by train on a wet morning in the spring of 2008 and walked from the station into the old centre of the city. It is a dispiriting quarter of a mile: a confusion of hotel signs; heavy traffic squeezing pedestrians on to the narrow pavements; booths selling trashy memorabilia; tourists with backpacks, hiking gear, leisure wear – suggesting how they regard one of the greatest original centres of urban civilization.

I wandered past the famous sites, watching teams of visitors being marched into the Duomo, queuing in front of the Palazzo Vecchio, ignoring the statue of David (which everyone knows is a replica). My morning was my own, but I had no inclination to look at works of art. I sat gloomily in a café, wondering about why visitors come here, and in such numbers. What do they want? Why do so many people crowd into the Uffizi, to gaze for a moment at the austere aristocratic formality of a religious painting by Andrea del Sarto, or stand briefly before the firm, lithe grace of a Botticelli?

My worst ever experience in a gallery was, in fact, in the Uffizi, while I was leading a group round Florence, a quick stop on a highlights-of-Europe tour. In the Tribune – an octagonal room hung with magisterial, unrelentingly noble portraits by Bronzino – a walkway had been set up. As the stream of visitors pressed on, those in front were forced to shuffle forwards, as if on a conveyor belt.

Memories like this invite the thought that such tourism is a deception: the crowds have been tricked into an empty veneration of the luxurious entertainments of their masters. The aspiring masses are tranquillized, and fleeced, as they stumble pointlessly past the objects whose real meaning is entirely lost upon them. My group went into the Duomo for half an hour, just long enough for me to explain that it was very difficult to build the dome, that it is 463 steps to the top (or something like that; I don't care) – they were fairly impressed by that number anyway until someone pointed out that it is hundreds less than the Eiffel Tower – and that the pattern on the floor is a kind of maze. They liked that last bit.

As I drink my coffee I am struck by the gap between the sincerity, the open goodwill, of those people I took round the buildings and galleries of Florence, and the misdirection of their admiration. It is not particularly interesting that the floor of a church is patterned like a maze; but perhaps it hit home precisely because it was simple; an almost childish thing among all that daunting age and distant power of the great works. Ironically it was the reputation of the great works that had drawn them to Florence in the first place. Who in their right mind would travel halfway round the world to see a floor set with a mildly intriguing pattern?

The person who buys a plastic six-inch model of David, or an I ♥ FIRENZI bumper sticker, is paying tribute to something they are excited by but cannot properly engage with. My melancholy memory is of genuine enthusiasm floundering around, seeking something, anything, to latch on to. The fame of the place is abstract, an indeterminate aura. My tour group wanted to be there but did not have a clue what to do with the pictures, statues, buildings and histories on which the reputation of the place rests. They came seeking something wonderful – a life-enhancing, life-transforming experience. But the explicit result was low-grade surprise. On a memorable occasion, as we were leaving Paris, one of my group asked an essential question: 'That *Mona Lisa* now, what's meant to be so great about it?' And then gave his own explanation: 'It's five hundred years old.' The question is the right one; the well-meaning answer is going nowhere. As his wife pointed out, there are many much older paintings.

Places like Florence and the Louvre are thought of as privileged centres of civilization; if we want to encounter civilization, surely it is to these sorts of places that we should come. Such motives certainly influenced the members of my group. But their confused responses reveal that merely visiting is not enough. What else needed to happen?

Having lingered as long as I dare in the café I head off for lunch. Fifteen minutes by taxi from the centre of Florence, in the suburb of Fiesole, is the Villa I Tatti (the 'I' and 'i' are both pronounced 'ee'). From the 1890s to the 1950s the villa was the home of Bernard Berenson. In his day BB, as he was called by his intimates, was the most famous art historian in the world and the first American scholar to make an indelible mark on an emerging discipline that had been, up to that point, a European preserve. My official reason for visiting was to examine some letters held in the fine library, from *Civilization* Clark to Berenson. (They were dull.)

BB was influential in shifting educated attention from

Rome and Venice, Raphael and Titian, to Florence, Giotto and Botticelli. At the end of the eighteenth century, for example, Goethe scarcely noticed Florence during his long wanderings in Italy. An Edwardian parlour game that is still played in sedate country houses after dinner is called 'Botticelli'. It is based on cultural knowledge, the archetypal question is: 'Name an Early Renaissance painter starting with B.' It is one of those tiny scraps of social history that can be traced back to thrilling intellectual and spiritual adventures; specifically, to the effective proselytizing of Berenson.

In Muriel Spark's novel, Miss Jean Brodie asks her girls to name the greatest Italian painter. One innocently suggests Leonardo da Vinci. No – says Miss Brodie, 'no, the greatest Italian painter is Giotto'. She is re-enacting – in an Edinburgh classroom in 1937 – a change of taste initiated forty years before by BB.

After graduating in Oriental Languages from Harvard, Berenson was supported by benefactors to make a trip to Rome, where he lived with the utmost frugality. 'I first came to Rome' – he wrote in a late travel journal – 'in the Autumn of 1888 and spent the following months on my feet from early morning to bedtime. Café latte cost me five soldi. Often had no lunch but munched roasted chestnuts and found them very comforting, and in my pocket they warmed my hands . . . I slept in the studio of an acquaintance who rented a trestle bed to me.'

In those days – he was in his early twenties – he devoted his time to looking and looking at works of art. A 'habit of adoration' was in formation. It was a habit that stayed with him all his life. Aged almost ninety he still writes rapturously of a small panel painted by Botticelli depicting a woman with her head in her hands sitting on a stone bench outside a massive palace, its great doors emphatically closed: 'its expression of utter abandonment penetrated me to the depths of the soul'. Here is his motive, here is the final purpose of scholarship for Berenson. The pursuit of knowledge serves the purpose of depth – not the extent or completeness or systematic organization of information, but the experience of being 'penetrated . . . to the depths of the soul'.

In 1896, at the age of thirty, Berenson published what was to be his magnum opus: *The Florentine Painters of the Renaissance*. It is a curious work because of its division into two dramatically different parts. The first part of the book is a long essay on aesthetics, discussing the central artistic achievements of the major Florentine painters. Berenson argues that the essence of pictorial art lies in the evocation of material reality through the deployment of two-dimensional properties. Thus the rendition of what he calls 'tactile values' is the key to painting. The artist (according to Berenson) seeks to convey the impression that we could touch – and hence know as real – the objects depicted. This is actually rather sophisticated and ranks as a permanent insight into realistic depiction. But behind this lies a larger topic: the attempt to define the 'higher' value of art and to discriminate better and worse ways of engaging with art.

The second part of the book is taken up with lists of attributions. For each painter, great or minor (or, as he casually puts it, scraping the bottom, 'tenth-rate'), he lists all the works he can recognize in public and private collections.

Berenson saw the leading Florentine painters as great individuals stamping their personality upon their works. Thus the point of attribution is to assign a work to a personality. And the rationale for attribution is the recognition of the stamp of that personality. Berenson took himself to be identifying the central artistic merit of a work and then using that to assign it to its author. So it is not at all that, knowing this is a Titian, we then see it as finer and deeper than we did before. But, seeing it as fine and deep in a very specific way, we are recognizing its kinship with other works – and they are all the works of Titian.

In other words, the lists and the painstaking scholarship serve a noble and humane end. The lists derive from, and encode, artistic merit. The hierarchy is clear. The scholarly work is important only because – and only to the extent that – it contributes to a wonderful experience. And the delighted encounter with a beautiful, lovely thing has many aspects that are not dependent upon scholarship. Berenson was excited by the sense of material weight and physical reality he found in a painter like Giotto, the founding figure of Florentine painting. Berenson was moved by the way in which we see Giotto's figures as real. But he did not learn this by looking things up in his library or by working in archives. His eyes told him. His eyes and his willingness to pay attention to his own experience. He was asking himself, as he stood in front of the frescoes: How is this work affecting me? Why do I find it appealing? What is the secret of its power?

In his musings on the nature and value of art, in his attempts to summarize the significance of the Renaissance (which he saw as the youth of humanity – a time of joy in life and excited self-discovery, of happy display and playfulness), Berenson opens himself to contention. But the significance of his way of discussing art does not lie in its philosophical truth, but in his attempt to explain why such knowledge matters. For Berenson it was a living question:

Why is the Renaissance important? How can it live in modern life? What does it offer us?

With these impressions of Berenson on my mind I wonder to what extent his legacy lives on. In his will, Berenson left the villa, the library and many pictures to Harvard University. I Tatti then became the home of the Harvard Center for Italian Renaissance Studies, eminent in the academic world both for its scholarly ideals and economic resources. But what is the prevalent idea of Renaissance Studies? What is it to study the Renaissance, and why – if one can dare to ask, where better to – is it a worthwhile field of inquiry? Bluntly, but honestly, you might ask: What do these people want to know, and why?

24

Up at the Villa

It is time to gather for a drink before lunch. We meet up in Berenson's old sitting room – which is suddenly filled with the twenty or so stipendiary scholars who are spending a year at I Tatti, mainly postdoctoral students in their late twenties, earlier thirties, with a few more senior academics present too. I wonder anxiously whether I can ask for a gin and tonic, but it is tomato juice all round – afternoons are for working. The sitting room on the ground floor, looking out over a small, not very formal, garden, has the elegant, beautifully mellow comfort that was so important to Berenson.

We do not linger and soon the director leads us through to the large dining room, set up with a single long table; there is no ostentation – no explicit grandeur – here. One of my enduring fantasies has always been to imagine living in a museum; not just camping out among the pictures and statues, but actually setting up home: doing all the things you cannot do in a gallery – have lunch, go to sleep, lie on a sofa and read a book, watch television, open a bottle of wine. But this is precisely what is done at I Tatti. It is all too easy to imagine a different history for this place; one in which it was turned into a museum, in which there would be ropes and barriers. You would be taken on a tour and the guide would tell you lots of well-meaning anecdotes but not let you look quietly, musing on your own reactions.

As the soup is served, the director, sitting at the head of the table, tells me a little about the research topics of the scholars who are now breaking bread, unfolding napkins, pouring water and serving each other half-glasses of estate wine. He explains something of his own research. He's been studying the legs of camels in pictures of the Magi: the wise men of the East who are depicted visiting the infant Christ in the stable at Bethlehem in many Renaissance paintings. Sometimes the camels' legs are crossed, sometimes they are not.

When the main course is placed before us, I try out an old strategy of inquiry: one most vigorously pursued by St Augustine. Why, he asked of the results of scholarly investigation, is it good to know that? There is – obviously – an infinite amount we can know about the world. Quantity is not the problem. But why do we want to know and, more pertinently, why is it good to know such things? Augustine was in search of a principle of quality – a principle that would help us see what, out of the infinite variation of possible knowledge, it was important to devote one's time and effort to.

Using Augustine as cover, I raise my question. It is one that seems so vital to me; one that always leaves hanging over my own life the possibility that, in the end, I have misdirected it. Why is it good to do research into the Renaissance? What are they hoping to discover? Why is it important? My inquiry falls flat. Perhaps I merely mistimed it: pressing it at the moment when others were selecting their meat from the communal plate and negotiating with the salad. But I sense a deeper reluctance; a coolness that might naturally meet an impertinent, unkind, unsavoury question – as if to sidestep would be, in the circumstances, the better option: to pretend that one had not actually heard a heartless or rude remark.

In a civilized investigation, the purpose – the human worth – of the task remains in view. For it is only when we have a sense of what we are trying to achieve that we can tell whether we are directing our efforts appropriately or not. But it is not merely that any purpose or aim is held up; rather that the point is open to serious reflection.

The vision of art appreciation that I sense is prevalent around the table places great emphasis upon knowledge. To be good at engaging with art is essentially to be in possession of a great deal of information; information that has to be acquired by diligent study – of which the assembled company are the high priests or, more modestly, the worker bees. Curiously, this seems to be the same attitude evident, at a much less elevated level, on guided tours back in the centre of the city.

It is a painful, dangerous thought. Perhaps it is precisely here, in the most august, most serious and best endowed institute, that we can see the cause of the confusion down in the city. The problem lies in the model of scholarship so assiduously and selflessly pursued by the pleasant, refined people up at the villa. For what they do is valorize arcana. They of course see themselves as ultimately working in the service of the love of art. But there is a striking disproportion between the effort and the vision: the labour that goes into the detail of research is unremitting; reflection upon why it is worth doing is occasional and fleeting – and not at all demanding. It is as if the question that initially motivated Berenson – Why is the Renaissance still important? – has been set aside. The tourists in the city are motivated, by and large, by the hope that in the galleries of Florence they will encounter something that will matter deeply to them. But the model of how to engage with the works in question derives from the scholars. And that is the problem.

It is not merely that the scholarly route is too long – too meandering and slow a path to enlightenment and fulfilment. It is rather that it has taken off on its own, paying occasional tribute to the idea that somehow in the end all of this knowledge will finally come alive in experience, but in reality serving no higher end than the accumulation of information for its own sake. This is a distressing example of a misguided ideal pursued vigorously by well-intentioned people.

Sitting opposite me, on the other side of the institute's director, is a young postdoctoral student. She is charming, clever and serious. But what will she devote her life and abilities to – as far as work is concerned? What is the trajectory of her ambition? My concern is that she will be gripped by an image of scholarship and will devote herself to finding out obscure facts about the past. It must look very tempting – the dignity of such a project seems guaranteed by the loveliness and discreet opulence of our surroundings. And yet I fear that this is a terrible waste, that it bypasses the real task.

I Tatti ought to be a creative centre of civilization – and the reasons it fails in that noble task are instructive. It studies the past in minute detail. But it does nothing to help us learn from, emulate or equal the achievements of the Renaissance. How could we, today, learn to build cities as dignified and inspiring as old Florence? How could we now cultivate the arts so that they would occupy as powerful and illuminating a place in modern culture as they did five hundred years ago in Italy?

These questions go to the heart of the value of the past, but they are out of bounds at the villa. It is dedicated to a sort of unconscious pessimism. I'm sure that the scholars there love what was best about the Renaissance. They love its buildings, paintings, ideas, music and literature. But they have no sense that such love should be a force in the present – a creative force guiding what we build and paint and write and compose and speculate about now. What we love about the past ought to be productive in the present.

The villa presents – in condensed form – a core problem of modern civilization. By definition, civilization is a long-term enterprise. And a key feature of the success of a civilization is how it renews the best aspects of its own history. This is the grand task of accumulation. The Renaissance is much admired, but its lessons are not part of our present-day culture. It is invoked in trivial ways. Patronage of any sort is thought of as today's version of the Medici – who were responsible for so much of the flowering of Florence. But what is so potent and impressive about Renaissance patronage is not the money that was spent (all ages spend money on the arts). What is striking is how well the money was spent – how it led to the creation of works that are still loved and admired around the world.

The most obvious lesson of the Renaissance is the determination to put the past to work in the present: to learn from and match the greatest achievements of the ancient world – to get back to the highest level. It is a revealing irony that the leading place in the world for studying the Renaissance should have no interest in that lesson. It is tragically – and unwittingly – in direct opposition to the spirit of the things it loves.

*

This is the point where, I believe, we start to make sense of the real civilizing mission. It is to do with trying to transmit what you love: not just to explain and make an assertion – although those might be good enough starting points. Transmission is something else. It is formative: it gets inside us and changes who we are. It is when you discover you can hear in a piece of music what another hears; that you can see what is so lovable about a particular picture; when an ideal or a longing jumps the gap between people and grows from one life to another.

I have been looking at the study of the Renaissance – in its currently unambitious form – for a specific reason. The idea of renaissance has been desperately missing from the art of modernity. That is, the idea that one can look to the past and find ideal achievements worth emulating; and so one can learn from and continue the best that has been made.

The solution is tantalizing, simple and cheap. The scholars need to move from the secondary historical question (What can we find out about the Renaissance?) to the primary philosophical question: What is it important to learn from the Renaissance that we could and should use today and that matters in the lives of many more people?

25

Depth

Civilization, I have been arguing, is closely connected to spiritual prosperity. But that phrase is more suggestive than explicit. What does it mean?

The word 'spiritual' needs some clarification. It is intended to refer to the whole of a person's inner life – it is intended to get away from talking only about an individual's intellectual abilities: their degree of cleverness or the extent of their knowledge. It includes how things go emotionally, what sorts of attitudes they have, the character of their imagination and memory. This is what we are getting at when we talk about someone's spirit – something you notice and recognize in a child or a friend: it is about their way of being, their soul.

We need not take 'spiritual' to entail a parallel and distinct non-material order of existence, harbouring exotic beings such as angels and demons, gods and ghosts. It names a set of complex properties that material creatures have. Religions, cults and myths are attempts – for better or worse – to organize and guide our inner lives. But the issue of spiritual life can be raised and pursued apart from religion. This matters because a conception of civilization – today – must be neither hostile to religion nor rely upon it.

To give the idea of spiritual prosperity more substance

I want to examine three key metaphors we often use to say that things are going well with someone's inner life: *depth* of thought, feeling or experience; attachment to *higher* things; and mental *space* or *breadth* of mind.

'Depth' is a word we appeal to when we need to signal something important, but don't quite know how to do it. There is a striking instance of this in a recent book by the engaging polemicist Steven Johnson entitled *Everything Bad is Good for You*.

Johnson argues – convincingly – that the image of popular culture as simple and simple-minded is inaccurate. He notes the complexity of certain computer games: the sheer amount of information that players have to deal with. He considers the intricacy of plotting that governs some television series. He argues that the ability to follow complex plots and deal with a lot of information are signs of intelligence. The plot lines of *The Simpsons* are just as intricate as the plot lines of Tolstoy's *War and Peace* or George Eliot's *Middlemarch*, two of the most highly regarded novels ever written (though, obviously, the cartoon is much funnier).

But then Johnson alludes to a huge issue that – otherwise – he carefully avoids. He breezily concedes that, in the end, what is impressive about Tolstoy or George Eliot is not the difficulty of their writing. Their works might have quite a lot going on in them – as do the instructions for making a Meccano crane or playing a computer game or mastering a chess opening. Many tasks are cognitively complex and it is good that we get smart about dealing with them. But, after all, what people have tended to admire about *Middlemarch* is not that it is informationally dense (like a street directory, or a legal contract), but that it is tremendously insightful; it has intellectual grace and dignity. And all this, he admits, is a wholly different issue. As he puts it: 'Some works are deep.'

The notion of depth occurs in connection with understanding and explanation. The surface phenomena are accounted for by way of a more powerful but hidden principle; and behind that may lie still deeper, more powerful and more general principles. This is often enough what happens when we come to understand something: we see the underlying point that explains the surface. Pursued systematically, this is science. So here, depth is the outcome of curiosity: the longing to go behind the veil and discover the secret causes of things.

The gateway to depth, therefore, is the word 'why'. *Why* is this good? *Why* is it important? *Why* do you believe that? *Why* do I love this thing? Each asks for an answer that – if given sincerely – reaches down into the causes and explanations of value.

Another, equally important, use of 'depth' is psychological: there are aspects of ourselves which when discovered seem particularly important and real but which are often ignored or passed over; perhaps because it takes time and imagination to discern them. There is a sense of getting to know someone deeply and of being known deeply.

When something goes deep with you it becomes central to your experience. It shapes and colours your vision of the world; it leaves its mark on your future.

These two strands of explanation and intimacy feed into the full idea of depth and shed light upon encounters in which something moves us deeply. For example, in Mozart's opera *Così fan Tutte* there is a moment when two young women are saying farewell to their sweethearts. The men are pretending to be about to sail off to join the army – although this is just a ploy to test the fidelity of the women. The audience are in on the plot and can easily guess the outcome: the vows of eternal love will soon be broken.

As the boat sails away, the women sing an especially lovely aria which starts with the words 'blow, gentle breezes'. It is an elemental plea: that the world should be generous and protective to those we love, that the sea be calm, the plane not crash; our wishes are, we know, beside the point: the wind cannot hear. Yet it is so normal and decent to want this – and it would not be an advance in humanity to treat this plea coldly. The music does not mock; it captures perfectly the purity of these fragile hopes.

In saying I find this deep I'm trying to get at the way it touches me; it seems to encapsulate a lot of other half-articulated longings and fears and thoughts about life – and, as it were, condenses them into a single representative moment, so that it has huge resonance while being simple. This makes the experience sound too intellectual; it is also that it returns me to something basic in myself which I am always forgetting or brushing aside. An experience of depth joins the summing-up aspect with the getting-under-the-skin aspect.

The aria touches the core of our emotional existence and is at the same time intellectually powerful. It brings the intensity of secret longing together with clarity and precision. It expresses a beautiful ideal: that thought and feeling can attract and illuminate one another and, finally, fuse.

Where does the experience of depth come from? One source is a kind of failure: we can feel at odds with and defeated by our external circumstances. Being unable to compete or hold one's own or thrive in the external world through physical prowess, strategic cunning, strength or allure of character, one turns inwards and makes a secondary, compensating realm of value which is moderately independent of external validation. And in this inner realm, the order of values can be the reverse of those that prevail in the wider world. And that is a source of strength because it provides a vantage point upon, and a place of safety from, the ways of the world.

Isaiah Berlin talked of 'a spiritual retreat' that generates a sense of depth – he saw it as particularly active in Germany in the very early stages of the Romantic Movement. He describes an extreme version of a fairly normal type of sensitive recoil from the harshness of the world. 'If you cannot get what you want, you must teach yourself to want what you can get. You try to lock yourself up against all the fearful ills of the world. The king of my province confiscates my land: I do not want to own land. The king does not wish to give me rank: rank is trivial, unimportant. The king has robbed me of my possessions: possessions are nothing.' Pressure builds up on the inner life, because that is something that remains to the individual.

This joins up with a more ordinary story: it is not so hard in individuals to trace a particular enrichment and deepening of the inner world via a degree of painful vulnerability: shyness, the child alone in the playground, humiliation and disappointment, loss and suffering can play an important part in the development of an individual's inner world and life (and hence the inner world acts as a kind of compensation). While none of this necessarily points to depth as being a suspect notion, it does perhaps reveal something of how it can be a bit threatening as an idea because it is at odds with breezy social virtue: the ideal of the bubbly team-player.

A good civilization cultivates, protects and guides the experience of depth and gives it weight in the world: such as, for example, when law develops so as to take into account a person's intentions and seeks to grasp what they were trying to do, not only what they actually did; when attention is given to qualities like remorse and recognition of guilt – when a person accepts that they have done something wrong and laments the wrong they have done; and when hope of redemption is held out. All of these are, in the field of law, indicators of the absorption of the idea of depth into a civilization.

But there are many things that can go wrong with depth – as it opens up a force that does not necessarily get well used in a person's life. These are cases in which depth is actually at odds with – and not an avenue of – flourishing.

Two major problems of depth are sentimentality and self-absorption. Sentimentality occurs when an object is asked to bear too great a burden of meaning. The demand is real, only it is directed at an unsuitable object. When Princess Diana died she became the object of a sentimental cult: millions of people projected their deepest longings on to her: they wanted to find in her life and death the key to the meaning of their own life. To them, she became a friend and protector (although deceased), a symbol of innocence, betrayal, redemption and tragedy. These are all very good things to seek. But choosing one person as a repository for all that yearning, and placing flowers wrapped in plastic in tribute to them, are signs of spiritual need: all that longing seeking somewhere to go and expressing itself in an inarticulate manner. The task of civilization is not to harden our hearts; on the contrary, it is to help our tender longings find their true targets.

Self-absorption is ineffective inwardness. The individual is aware of the endless recesses of their personality. But they cannot make use of them in life other than as a means of temporary escape.

The civilizing of inner life – the cultivation and education of depth – is the task of expression. Depth seeks expression. Expression is not just letting off steam – or letting out an inner condition; the process of expression turns an inner state into an external or public object.

One clue to the nature of expression can be found in some lines from a poem by Gerard Manley Hopkins:

> Margaret, are you grieving
> Over Goldengrove unleaving?
> Leaves, like the things of man, you
> With your fresh thoughts care for, can you?
> Ah! As the heart grows older
> It will come to such sights colder
> . . .
> And yet you will weep and know why
> . . .
> It is Margaret you mourn for.

The critical lines are the last two. Discovery of the real and often personal source of grief enriches the emotion. And this is one of the central tasks of expression: that the source of feeling be found.

For a second clue to expression, consider the Requiem written by Berlioz in 1837, in particular the second part, which is a setting of some lines from a medieval Latin poem, the *Dies Irae* – the day of wrath – which describe the end of the world and the Day of Judgment. In a sense, Berlioz's music – among the grandest ever written – performs the same function as the plastic-wrapped flowers outside the gates of Kensington Palace. Both show how someone feels. But the music speaks of the terror of death, and the fear of a life wasted, with a much greater awareness of the scale and depth of those emotions. The plastic wrappers are prompted by the same feelings – but the feelings cannot be carried by them; the wrappers are desperate to say something, but cannot say it. The music sings of the immensity of fear, loss and hope.

In expression, a fugitive inner state is given completion and hence can be, perhaps for the first time, seen and known; an inner state is given security by being located in the outer world; we can return to it and have a different kind of access to it; expression allows another person to recognize and identify with inner life; hence expression is linked to fulfilment and belonging.

Obviously expression is not confined to grief. Any area of inner life can be developed through the twin aspects of expression: recognition of the real source of feeling and articulation of its character and meaning. How a house is built, furnished and lived in; how a dinner is given; how a garden is planted and tended and enjoyed; how a holiday is planned and taken: all of these can and should be expressive; they are all ways in which our inward longings and needs can find their proper homes in the world.

In any ambitious form of expression there is a huge dependence upon material resources and upon the capacity to actually control those resources: building plots, wine glasses, mortgages, airline tickets, saplings, cooking pots. And also, of course, the time and effort and education required to gain mastery of an art form. In other words, depth is where expression starts; its fulfilment requires technical skill – the ability to deploy material resources. The expression of love in a holiday, a home, a meal, requires two kinds of aptitude: an emotional depth and also the practical capacity to put this into action in the world.

This is one of the points where we can trace the intimate connections between spiritual prosperity and material prosperity, which is a natural characteristic of expression.

In 1517 Pope Leo X (a member of the Medici family) issued an indulgence to provide funds for continuing work on the new St Peter's in Rome. The decision to tear down the old St Peter's and rebuild on the grandest possible scale had been taken decades before by Pope Julius II – with Bramante as the principal architect. The idea behind an indulgence was that by paying for one the individual received remission for their sins. There was a relatively decent rationale for this: it was clearly good to give money to support the work of the Church, and to do a good deed of this kind must surely count for something in the moral balance of one's life.

But in practice, the balance had been unduly formalized and made into an industry. Thus those who gave permission for an indulgence to be sold in their territory could take a cut of the proceeds. People readily believed that buying an indulgence (the mere financial transaction) on its own was sufficient to make up for cruel, selfish or immoral actions. This contrasted rather unfavourably with the more serious attitude of people who tried hard to behave well in the first place – those who struggled against temptation, who sought to control their desires, who were willing to forgo pleasures or satisfactions for the sake of an ideal.

One such person was a German monk, a professor at

the University of Wittenberg (in Saxony), Martin Luther. Luther was demanding on himself: 'I tried as hard as I could to keep the Rule of my religious order and made lists of my sins. I confessed them again and again. I scrupulously carried out the penances which were allotted to me. And yet my conscience kept nagging. It kept telling me: "You fell short there." "You were not sorry enough." "You left that sin off your list."' To a man with such an ardent sense of his own failing, and such a serious vision of what would be required to put things right (self-transformation), the idea of buying an indulgence, of handing over some cash and setting all to rights with your moral life, seemed not just mistaken – not just an intellectual or conceptual error – but totally opposed to the real business of life. Luther was, unsurprisingly, drawn to the writings of St Augustine. Augustine too had battled with his conscience, had lived through agonies of remorse. One lesson that Luther drew from this was that merely 'external' actions do not count for much. Everything depends upon the feelings and attitudes of the 'inner' man.

Luther is a representative figure in the discussion of civilization. That is because he is a hero of the demand for authenticity. Luther is a great rejector of fake visions of higher things. He cannot bear that people should get excited about a relic – about the shoe that belonged to a saint. It is not because he hates shoes per se but because he views the act of investing faith in such an object as the enemy – the internal enemy – of a more genuine relationship. And this lesson is overwhelmingly important today. We live in a society that would have driven Luther mad. Although we are probably less inclined to worship holy footwear – it is only the objects of devotion that have changed: their misguided nature remains.

Our private reformation is always in progress: the desire to strip away the useless parts and be loyal to what seems most serious. What was so impressive about Luther was the way he managed to transmit his own earnestness to others. His longing to be true to himself and not to go along with what seemed to him shabby and misguided started out as utterly private: a battle in himself conducted entirely alone. But it quite quickly became apparent that Luther was a representative figure: his inner ambition for authenticity illuminated the longings of others.

BERNINI

The construction of St Peter's was completed in the second half of the seventeenth century, under the direction of Bernini – he designed the huge colonnades, took responsibility for the interior, and enhanced the approaches to the Vatican from the centre of Rome. This is the image of external grandeur, spreading out from an intense core to civilize the world. There is a painful tension between the images of life we find in Luther and Bernini. Luther stands for the absolute centrality of the inner life – honesty, self-examination, humility. Bernini stands for glory, confidence and the dramatic realization of these qualities in grand architectural statements. And yet the two seem to be in opposition. The very qualities that Luther stands for lead to visual banality, to a kind of anxious modesty which sees grandeur as merely pretentious. And yet the architecture of Bernini can easily seem heartless and inhumane. Luther is the apostle of individualism – each private person must make their own version of the truth, and must hold on to that more vigorously than to anything else. The achievement of Bernini requires the subordination of individualism – the coherence and consistency of the huge undertaking requires that the individual will be moulded to it – people cannot come along and seek to express their private view of things. Architects must be made to obey a single vision; artists and decorators must follow the single overall conception. (Although it is important to recollect that this is an extremely noble overall conception.)

Bernini is an example of a crucial aspect of civilization: together with his patron, he stands for the compelling material expression of our inner needs and ambition. This has been pursued in many ways, but Bernini's colonnades – and the whole baroque vision that is made real in them – are outstanding representatives of the task.

Together, Luther and Bernini help us identify an elemental project of civilization: to combine the demand for authenticity – for individual sincerity and personal intimacy – with the demand for the powerful outward display of values.

26

Higher Things

If we are feeling ground down by petty or trivial issues – overtaken by banality – we might go in search of 'higher things': somehow the reverse of trivial; but these words do not really tell us what we are looking for. So, can we get some insight into the idea of higher things?

Perhaps the metaphor starts in a real experience: climbing a hill or a tower, you literally rise above your surroundings, you see things from a new and quite revealing angle; 'higher things' would suggest a psychological equivalent of this; some internal equivalent of climbing a hill or going up a tower.

In Western philosophy, the most ambitious account of higher things – what they are and why they matter – is to be found in the works of Plato. In the *Phaedrus*, a discussion of the nature of true love, Plato has Socrates describe the human condition. We are, he says, souls that have shed their wings and fallen to earth. We retain, however, a dim and distant memory of our earlier being. By devoting ourselves to those things on earth that bear a likeness to the original perfection, we raise ourselves up and begin our journey home. 'Beauty, wisdom and goodness are the prime sources of nourishment and growth to the wings of the soul; but their opposites, such as ugliness and evil, cause the wings to waste and perish.'

This myth suggests something important. One key element in the experience of higher things is the idea of feeling uplifted: it is as if you are actually rising or swelling (perhaps music gives the best instances of this). In this uplift, you encounter yourself in a new way: you feel cleaner, more heroic, more powerful, more noble than usual – and, curiously, this unusual sensation is experienced as 'how things ought to be', as more real, and more true to one's nature, than more familiar and common states of being.

The proper names for higher things are 'goodness' and 'beauty'. And the relevant experience is of 'love': in which we have an unusually pure apprehension of what beauty and goodness are and of our need for them.

Moments when this might occur: alone in a darkened chapel; light coming through the trees; the far horizon at sunset: these are events that make us noble, but their fineness and significance are hard to contain in an ordinary life, and they are horribly threatened with corrupt versions and grim associations which get in the way of understanding them. So there is a feeling of having to be a bit quiet about this.

You might be driving home in the early evening in spring. You are struck by the light – both strong and soft. You turn off your usual route and park by a public garden and go for a walk under some large trees. The light through the branches, the freshness of the air, the silvery edge to everything, the tranquillity of the sky: this gives you an acute sense of beauty and loveliness; and in being open to it, in feeling a hunger for it, you feel that this ought to be more central to your life. This kind of experience ought to have dominion: you should reorganize your life to find more of this (get up early, go for walks, pay more attention to trees and the sky). Cities ought to be reorganized to encourage and support such experiences; people should stop work for half an hour before sunset on sunny days.

Higher things are connected with ideals: that is, with pictures of perfection, with goals and eventual outcomes. An ideal is more than a daydream, more than just what we happen to want. An ideal is cast as something one ought to want; as having a claim upon us. It comes as a demand, as a call, not just as a preference. And that is part of the nature of higher things: that they exercise a claim upon us. There is a drama of doubt and assent and of acceptance.

We are taken up: subsumed into and absorbed by something that seems greater than ourselves, but in which we can participate – which is why we are enlarged; we share in the nature of the thing into which we are subsumed. In possessing an epic sense, we are not merely reading an epic, but coming to participate in one. In thrilling to grandeur, we become grand; in responding to serenity, it enters our souls and we become an extension of that serenity.

27

Mental Space

The third of the metaphors of spiritual prosperity, after 'depth' and 'higher things', is 'mental space'; with its kindred images of breadth and openness of mind.

In an essay, 'Tradition and the Individual Talent', of 1919, T. S. Eliot writes: 'No poet or artist has his complete meaning alone. His significance, his appreciation is the appreciation of his relations to the dead poets and artists.' And he continues: 'What happens when a new work of art is created is something that happens simultaneously to all the works of art that have preceded it. The existing monuments form an ideal order amongst themselves, which is modified by the introduction of the new (the really new) work of art among them. The existing order is complete before the new work arrives; for order to persist after the supervention of novelty, the *whole* existing order must be, if ever so very slightly, altered; and so the relations, proportions, values of each work of art towards the whole are readjusted.'

Eliot here gives voice to a point larger than his specific application of it to artistic creation. An open mind – we should say, inspired by this – is one that can be readjusted in the light of a new fact or idea. But there has to be this process, and there has to be something to be adjusted. This places a weight of responsibility on the new idea – that it can stand introduction into the existing order: that it has the power and the potency to call for and sustain a reordering. The finer the existing tradition (or the better furnished the individual mind) the larger this task becomes – the greater resistance to absorbing novelty for its own sake. The response to novelty becomes more exacting, more demanding – and rightly so.

What we see here is a statement about having an open mind. Eliot sees an open mind as one that can absorb new material into an existing and serious conception of the world. By contrast, being open-minded is often thought of merely in terms of receptivity – what you are willing to take in, with no concern about where that new material goes. This illuminates a standing problem of open-mindedness: readiness to accept anything, because it is new or different.

One of the things which may lead to the cultivation of mental space is ambivalence: that is, the condition of not being able to come down for or against something – of being torn in one's response – wanting, that is, to hang on to two things which do not fit at all well together. The solution – as it were – is to expand the inner space in which both can live.

The cultivation of mental space is the growth of the ability to live with ambivalence. Such growth sometimes has its origin in quite painful experiences. Consider a child who loves and is impressed by both parents but who is aware of quite bitter conflict between them. There is no chance of simply saying that one is right and the other wrong. There is a demand, here, to love and hold on to two ways of experiencing the world, two visions of what life is about; yet these ways are in conflict.

To speak personally: I was miserably aware all through my childhood of the dramatic ways in which my parents caused each other terrible anguish. It took a long time for me to realize that they did not do this deliberately; the mutual pain was the consequence of a divergence of intensely held convictions – convictions that coloured every aspect of their lives and were grounded in the deepest experiences they had had. My mother believed, at the core of her self, that the external circumstances of life counted for little; real life was what went on in your soul. Love was the absolute meaning of life – often given intense and profound expression in situations of suffering and depriv- ation. She would see in everyone the need for redemption and forgiveness – and the more outrageous the fault the more she would intuit a buried, desperate plea for love. A certain tone of voice and look of quiet trust was – for her – the summit of human goodness.

My father was moved by a vision of external beauty – he was deeply drawn to any physical object that had been made with care and ingenuity; he loved a finely made glass, a well-balanced silver fork, the rough texture of a linen napkin; he was profoundly sensitive to the design of a chair, to the placing of pictures in a room, to the sound of a balanced engine, and the handling of a classic sports car. And he wanted the whole world to share this sensitivity: an ugly new building in a simple old street would stir him to an astonishing rage; political injustice of any sort would make his blood boil, and give rise to horrifying curses and oaths. Their opposed views on the largest questions of meaning came to be focused on tiny details of daily life.

What needs to happen is that the mental space of the growing child develops in order to be able to contain and hold on to these divergent and actually warring factions; as if the mind could become a house big enough for the parents to cohabit but not have to meet one another very much.

But mental space is not just about keeping things apart. I want to stress the labour of the mind that is necessary here. It is crucial to distinguish between an easy accommodation – an attitude of live and let live – and a different phenomenon. The labour that is involved comes from taking both sides seriously. It does not pretend that the two sit easily together; it does not accommodate both by neutering them and turning them into innocuous versions of themselves. (Although I do not deny that such strategies might be very helpful in emergencies.)

A much more public version of this might come when one is faced with rivalry and competition between people one admires. In 1959 the British novelist, scientist and high-ranking public servant C. P. Snow (later Lord Snow) gave the annual Rede Lecture: at the time a truly national intellectual occasion.

Snow entitled his lecture 'The Two Cultures and the Scientific Revolution' and he spoke of a growing separation of the high culture of literature from the high culture of science. Scientists and those educated in the arts and humanities could not communicate seriously to each other: 'the intellectual life of the whole of Western society is increasingly being split into two polar groups . . . at one pole we have the literary intellectuals . . . at the other the scientists.'

As a characteristic instance, Snow recalled a conversation in which some people, highly educated in the humanities, were lamenting the illiteracy of scientists. He asked if they could describe the Second Law of Thermodynamics. 'The response was cold: it was also negative. Yet I was asking something which is about the scientific equivalent of: Have you read a work of Shakespeare?'

Snow was on to something important: how can different sophisticated parts of a culture talk to each other? And he saw the problem not just as a simple misfortune – but more deeply as a resistance and a disdain on both sides. He was encountering sophisticated scholars of the humanities who did not really want to know about what was happening in the sciences, let alone about what was really happening in business or government. Wanting to know is quite different from making demands.

Yet the same could be said for the scientists. Or for those in government or business. I was drawn to Snow's novels precisely because they range widely over divergent fields of expertise: they deal with matters of law, science, the relationships between government and civil service; between industry and academic life; they are concerned with the process of ageing, with the nature of responsibility and of choice.

A contemporary of Snow was the literary critic F. R. Leavis. I had been much impressed by his book *The Great Tradition*, in which he discusses what he considers to be the major novels in English. Irrespective of one's agreement with his choice – I think it is a pretty good selection – what is impressive is how much he gets out of reading. His ideal is to enter sympathetically the imaginative world of the book and to evaluate that world from the point of view of one's own experience. How well, he keeps on asking, does this author understand life: its possibilities, difficulties, intricacies and beauty? How alive are they to the delicate texture of experience? And with what skill and tact are they able to convey this insight and understanding and sensitivity?

Leavis was intensely upset by Snow's lecture. He thought of Snow as a 'portent': an advance warning of all that would soon go wrong with civilization. He described Snow as 'someone who thinks of himself as a novelist' but whose stories do not deserve that title. He was appalled by a culture that could regard Snow as a wise and learned man.

This was difficult for me to hear. Here were two highly impressive people – heroes I felt drawn to. They did not merely disagree; they were in bitter conflict. It is not surprising that people disagree; the difficulty I had here was deeper. Both men make a claim upon one's loyalty to a view of life. And one cannot respond to both. Snow presented a vision of adaptability – of adjustment to the ways of the world, so that one could follow a career, get on and make money, wield influence and attain honour in the public eye. Leavis cannot stand this attitude and sees it as dangerous and false. He pleads with his readers to resist. Everything important in life depends upon not being adaptable; in sticking absolutely to what is good, although this will involve being disregarded, passed over, regarded as a crank. That is the price it is necessary to pay.

This is not merely an interesting dispute – a stimulus to reflection, or an engaging combat, like a joust which one watches from afar. It is a dispute which can tear a life apart: Which side is one really on? Is it necessary to choose? This is a paragraph I cannot finish. I am searching for mental space and I cannot find it.

As a final instance of mental space, think of the photographs of, say, Berlin in the 1890s: the dapper people strolling the streets; block after block of elegant apartments – with their public dignity of classical columns and pediments while inside there are plenty of books and comfortable sofas and pianos; the inviting doors of the self-consciously sophisticated cafés. It is an image of urban life at its most alluring.

We know perfectly well the imperfections that some people are all too keen to remind us of: we know that it was a society with many defects, we know that a few streets away there is squalor, inequality and all the rest. But still, there is something those photographs are showing us that we are right to love.

But this love is mixed with another emotional pang, something more akin to pain. And the pain is not just to do with the fact that those particular buildings have been damaged, or that one will not be able to live in that apartment, pass through that doorway and saunter into that café to order a coffee. It is that we feel, that we know, that such a life is not possible. What then might have been a fairly widespread form of life – nothing terribly remarkable – would today be a vastly expensive affectation.

Nostalgia often gets a bad name. It is condemned as useless or sentimental – this tenderness can be mocked so as to make us feel out of date or guilty of some disloyalty to the modern world. But nostalgia is a form of love – and it is a conduit of understanding. It is naive, indeed unkind, to suppose that our nostalgia for some imagined past of civilization is a species of intellectual error. As if we simply forgot that the past was full of atrocities. Surely there is mental space enough in a civilized mind to love something without pretending that there was nothing wrong with it.

Nostalgia is a type of obscure knowledge: it offers us an insight into what we love. But it is a painful insight because we fear that what we love has already been lost and can no longer be retrieved. So, the pain is a kind of grief. Even if it is grief for an idea of something that was never quite as beautiful, nowhere near as perfect, in reality as it is in our minds. But such grief is not a failing: it is a largeness of spirit.

28

Our Sovereign Concept

The essence of civilization can be defined like this: Civilization occurs when a high degree of material prosperity and a high degree of spiritual prosperity come together and mutually enhance each other.

'Mutual enhancement' means that deep and noble attitudes guide consumption and the use of material resources. But it also means that spiritual prosperity is sympathetic to, and encouraging of, material prosperity.

An individual is civilized to the degree that this integration is accomplished in their life. But civilization depends upon this being widespread. A group of societies constitute a civilization in so far as they systematically and reliably help this integration, so that it becomes normal.

Such integration is not reserved for special occasions: it is revealed in the details of everyday life: how people talk and take their holidays; it is at work in our ideas of entertainment and dignity, in what cities look like and the workings of government.

There are (in principle) many ways in which the project of civilization can be carried out – because there is not just one realization for spiritual prosperity and because the realization depends upon the material circumstances of the day. But the pursuit of different versions of this project diminishes, rather than intensifies, the possible frictions and disputes between nations.

The critical factor, at the present time, is the greater strength of the pursuit of material prosperity, which has attained a degree of magnitude that outruns the spiritual resources of our time. However, it is no solution to this problem to seek to undercut or reduce the drive to material prosperity. The drive to material prosperity is deeply entrenched and so powerful that seeking to eliminate it is either fanciful or cruel. In any case, material prosperity is not in itself a problem. The problem is we have material prosperity (or had until recently) beyond our spiritual competence to deal with it well.

So the primary task that we are faced with is the development of spiritual prosperity in such a way that it can hold its own against the material drive.

Many of the large and urgent problems of today can be traced to this single, underlying issue. What do the following have in common? Global economic insecurity; the environment and climate change; the ugly sprawl of cities; the painful balancing act between the demands of work and meaning in life. Ultimately, each one points to a mismatch between two things we want: material prosperity and spiritual prosperity.

Here is the paradox. The entire global economy is geared to serving human desires: to creating goods and services that people want to buy. The market place is a vast mirror in which majority choices are displayed. Yet we are not really getting what we want: we are not terribly happy, the world is not beautiful and safe.

There has been a long, long fight between money and goodness. But there is no absolute reason why they must be enemies. There is a hesitancy here: could it really be that doing good could be profitable? But that is not to say that making profits – however you do it – is morally good; it means that we need being ethical and generous and noble and intelligent to be ways of making money. This is not to dirty these fine qualities by mixing them with sordid finance.

The humanities – history, philosophy, the classics, literature and the arts – are our collective treasure house of wisdom. But you might not think this, because mostly the treasure house is locked and bolted. The keepers of the treasure spend their time talking to one another. Instead of being beacons of spiritual prosperity they are bank vaults.

This is where business comes in. Business is not only to do with making profits. It is to do with facing competition, understanding the needs of your clients and customers and knowing what your strengths (and potential weaknesses) are.

Through the 1970s the big theme in business was the creation of desire. The essential message of advertising of the era was: 'We know what will make you happy.' The message was less than candid, because the subtext was: How can we get you to want the things that will make us rich?

Since the 1990s businesses have become more and more responsive to what people want. They aim to target more closely than their rivals exactly what people are willing to spend their money on, and to provide that more efficiently than their rivals. Now the essential message of advertising is: 'You know what will make you happy – and we are listening to you.'

But the opportunity for the future is going to lie in desire leadership. It marries the two earlier trends: creative leadership in influencing what people want; together with a service towards actual needs. The future of business lies in teaching people their real needs, not just fabricating new wants.

This is where the humanities come in. The underlying point of the humanities – often submerged by scholarship – has been the study of what it is good to desire – of what our real needs are. And this is the topic on which the most innovative businesses of the future will found their fortunes.

Business and the humanities can educate one another. And in so doing they can solve the greatest question of our age: How can money and goodness work together to make us happy?

A sovereign concept is one that stands at the pinnacle of a whole range of concerns and activities and describes what it is that – in the end – they are attempting to achieve. A sovereign concept exerts a downwards pressure; so that how you imagine happiness will influence what you think of as important, and will have more remote implications for the way you lead your life.

Civilization is a sovereign concept because it stands (that is, ought to stand – for often it has been missing) at the summit of thinking about many of the large areas of modern life and culture. Thus, the purpose of the economy is to promote civilization – to allow people to live civilized lives; the purpose of education is to promote civilization; the purpose of the arts and of entertainment, of science and of architecture, has the same final trajectory.

We should think of civilization as a project originating in the inner needs of individuals. These needs can be described in several interrelated ways: for spiritual prosperity; for happiness; for flourishing. But these needs are not exclusively, or purely, inner. That is, it is the nature of these needs that they require support from, and seek fulfilment in, the external world.

For example, happiness is an inner state of satisfaction. But the capacity to be happy depends upon support from the outer world – one needs education, opportunity, advice and encouragement. These support the achievement of an inner condition of happiness. But, further, that inner state seeks realization and expression in the outer world: the inner state projects itself outwards. A happy life is played out in the material world: making a good home for oneself and others; undertaking purposeful and decent work; the creation, care of and enjoyment of beauty.

To put this in a slightly less abstract way: a happy life is lived through the way you live, where you live, what you do, how you act out friendships and cope with responsibilities and difficulties.

Suger – at St-Denis – was such an important pioneer for civilization because of his way of combining, and yet keeping apart, idealist and realist attitudes. His idealism was evident in the way he held on to a vision of perfection: he wanted people to love what was fine and beautiful and intensely serious. His realism was evident in the way he recognized what people are often like (feckless, greedy, status seeking). He did not use his realism about what people are like to undercut his vision of where he wanted them to go. He did not end up saying that since people are like this, that is fine and who am I to say they should be any different? His idealism – and the gap it opens between perfection and the way things are – did not lead him to hate or despise people. He shows us how to link generosity and the pursuit of perfection.

A hero of civilization – like Suger or Cicero or Matthew

Arnold – is someone who is teaching us how to combine devotion to noble values with an acceptance of the ways of the world. They are heroes in my eyes because they do not seek to exploit whatever authority they might have; they accept that they have to do the work if they are to convince other people; they stand for kindness as well as wisdom.

Few images of civilized life are more evocative – or have had longer influence – than the Roman villa. In one of his letters, Pliny 'the Younger' describes his own villa. It is by the sea; one of the terraces opens on to a rocky bay – a good place for swimming. The grouping of the buildings is informal – and some of them are very simple – but there are touches of refinement, almost grandeur. A fine portico opens from the bay into an inner courtyard – sheltered from the winds; there are a few statues based on Greek models. (Pliny wrote a lot about these; it was thanks to his descriptions that during the Renaissance newly unearthed statues could be identified.) A couple of rounded loggias take advantage of the sea views; there is an orchard close to the house. The villa is large – being a working farm as well as a home; you could wander within it.

And the image of life the building supports is attractive too. Pliny wrote a good deal – factual, historical and loosely scientific works. But he was also involved in the practical business of farming; he wrote a lot of letters; he had a distinguished career in public service.

We have moved from the profoundly public concerns of Plato to a more private world. The villa does not pretend to be the model for a whole world, it is a limited domain – but within it, life can be civilized. We are far from the pessimism of Plato's good man sheltering behind the wall as the hailstones of life beat down.

The more philosophical aspect of the villa ideal is exemplified by Cicero – who makes one of his country places the setting for intellectual conversation (*Discussions at Tusculum*). It is not professional philosophy of the highest order; one could imagine Plato or Aristotle getting frustrated. But nor are the discussions trivial or ignorant; they are, rather, the high level of non-professional debate: the level at which, if at all, ideas work their way in the world.

Cicero combined a highly significant political career with a major interest in and service to philosophy. In *The Orator* – which is something of an idealized self-portrait – Cicero argues that the orator should not only have a technical competence (in the various rhetorical moves which can be made) but must also have a broad education; he must acquire wisdom and understand the nature of argument; that is, he must be involved in the pursuit of the truth. This shows a clear eye for practical outcomes; wisdom needs to be armed with eloquence so that it can have an effect in the world. Joking about one of the more high-minded Romans, Cicero comments – 'he [Cato] behaved as if he were living in Plato's republic rather than in the cesspool of Romulus'.

The educational model Cicero refers to is heavily indebted to Greece – to Plato, Aristotle and their intellectual heirs, the Epicureans and Stoics. Like most sophisticated Romans, Cicero took the culture of Greece very seriously but with a certain degree of ambivalence. For many Romans the most obvious fact about Greece was its military defeat – its subject status. And this qualified and limited their admiration. This was not an assertion of the crude belief that 'might is right'. Rather it was the serious worry that learning, refinement, conceptual sophistication and artistic achievement are not resilient. It is precisely because the Romans admired these achievements of the Greeks that they were disturbed by the military and political failure of the Greek states. And, also, why they thought that Rome had something valuable to offer. The ideal that people like Cicero entertained was of an integration of the refinement and cultivation of the Greeks with the robust military and administrative capacities of Rome.

Rome needed the philosophy of Greece – and Cicero was one of the major agents of this cultural project. Central to this project was Cicero's 'popularization' of philosophy. Not an original thinker, he took seriously the idea that for philosophy to have an impact on life it had to be presented in a way that could engage with people who would never be scholars – but who would be generals, governors and senators.

These classical examples matter to us today because they show two important things about the integration of material and spiritual prosperity. Pliny found a way of creating a cultured space in which he could be both an administrator and a thinker. And in making his domestic environment convivial and elegant, he spread his culture to others. Pliny was the living example of an ideal.

Cicero's version of this integration of intellectual and practical life focuses on communication. He is intently aware that the demands of practical life do not sit well with strenuous devotion to intellectual culture. The generals and statesmen are too busy – not too stupid – to read complex disquisitions on abstruse topics.

There is a story told by the literary critic Walter Benjamin that goes like this: There was a man who was devoted to books; he wanted to collect and possess them. But he was poor and could not afford to buy the volumes he wanted. He used to pick up catalogues from the booksellers and gaze longingly at the titles. And then he would set about making the books himself: writing the words that, he imagined, they might contain.

This story has a grander cousin, told of Picasso. When the great artist was young and not yet successful or wealthy, he would see paintings that he loved and coveted but could not afford. To bring hope and reality together he set about painting for himself in his own way the works he most admired.

These are two intertwined visions of creation arising out of unfulfilled love. The promise of civilization is robust: the opportunity does not disappear just because it is neglected. It may be that the books we read help awaken a longing for civilization, or give a special name to a need that we have caught sight of. But the fulfilment of that promise is written, if it is written at all, in another book we are all writing and which we recommence as we finish every final page: the book of life.

Acknowledgements

Thanking people can be an ambiguous matter. I am grateful to a number of individuals for their very real kindness and help. But I fear I have made poor use of what they have offered; I am ashamed to list the generous people who may at times have felt that they had cast their pearls before a swine.

However, on a very different note, I should like to record my special gratitude to Ian Renard, former Chancellor of the University of Melbourne, who has educated my view of the world.

The author and publisher wish to thank the following for their kind permission to reproduce copyright materal:

Extracts from 'Deftly, Admiral, Cast Your Fly' and 'As I Walked Out One Evening' by W. H. Auden, from *Collected Auden*, reproduced by permission of Faber & Faber Ltd.

Extract from 'The Love Song of J. Alfred Prufrock' by T. S. Eliot, from *Collected Poems, 1924–32*, reproduced by permission of Faber & Faber Ltd.

ACKNOWLEDGEMENTS

Extract from 1919 essay 'Tradition and the Individual Talent' by T. S. Eliot, reproduced by permission of Faber & Faber Ltd.

Extract from *A Room of One's Own* by Virginia Woolf, reproduced by permission of The Society of Authors as the literary representative of the Estate of Virginia Woolf.

John Armstrong

CONDITIONS OF LOVE: THE PHILOSOPHY OF INTIMACY

What does it really mean to love another person? Is there such a thing as the 'perfect partner'? How does infatuation differ from the real thing? The need to love and to be loved is central to our idea of happiness, yet it sometimes seems that the more we reflect on it the more elusive it becomes. In this lucid and graceful meditation on the deeper meanings of intimacy, John Armstrong explores the ideas that have shaped how we view affairs of the heart.

'Wise, discursive ... Powerful and valuable' *Sunday Times*

'The reader is attracted, amused, encouraged to respond, left fulfilled and eager for more' *Independent*

'Armstrong is perceptive and tender' *Evening Standard*

'Wryly right' *Guardian*

JOHN ARMSTRONG

THE SECRET POWER OF BEAUTY
WHY HAPPINESS IS IN THE EYE OF THE BEHOLDER

What is beauty? Does it exist in the proportions of a perfect face or a graceful melody, or is it in the eye of the beholder? Why does someone find beauty in an object that leaves others unmoved?

The notion of beauty is elusive: we love and seek out the things we find beautiful, yet it seems impossible to describe their essence. John Armstrong takes us on a lucid and lyrical exploration of beauty's power, tracing the various ways in which we have interpreted its secrets through art, literature and philosophy. In doing so he helps us deepen our own responses to beauty.

'Good soul food in a hungry age' *Herald*

'A romp through many incarnations of beauty – people, music, sculpture and architecture' *Observer*

He just wanted a decent book to read ...

Not too much to ask, is it? It was in 1935 when Allen Lane, Managing Director of Bodley Head Publishers, stood on a platform at Exeter railway station looking for something good to read on his journey back to London. His choice was limited to popular magazines and poor-quality paperbacks – the same choice faced every day by the vast majority of readers, few of whom could afford hardbacks. Lane's disappointment and subsequent anger at the range of books generally available led him to found a company – and change the world.

'We believed in the existence in this country of a vast reading public for intelligent books at a low price, and staked everything on it'
Sir Allen Lane, 1902–1970, founder of Penguin Books

The quality paperback had arrived – and not just in bookshops. Lane was adamant that his Penguins should appear in chain stores and tobacconists, and should cost no more than a packet of cigarettes.

Reading habits (and cigarette prices) have changed since 1935, but Penguin still believes in publishing the best books for everybody to enjoy. We still believe that good design costs no more than bad design, and we still believe that quality books published passionately and responsibly make the world a better place.

So wherever you see the little bird – whether it's on a piece of prize-winning literary fiction or a celebrity autobiography, political tour de force or historical masterpiece, a serial-killer thriller, reference book, world classic or a piece of pure escapism – you can bet that it represents the very best that the genre has to offer.

Whatever you like to read – trust Penguin.